LAWS
of the
ALAMANS
and
BAVARIANS

LAWS
of the
ALAMANS
and
BAVARIANS

Translated, with an Introduction,
by

THEODORE JOHN RIVERS

University of Pennsylvania Press

1977

Library of Congress Cataloging in Publication Data
Main entry under title:

Laws of Alamans and Bavarians.

   Translation of Leges Alamannorum and Lex
Baiuvariorum.
       Bibliography: p.
       Includes index.
       1. Law, Germanic.   I.   Rivers, Theodore John,
1944–   II.   Leges Alamannorum.   English.   1977.
III.   Lex Baiuvariorum.   English.   1977.
Law   340.5'5   77–81449
ISBN 0–8122–7731–7

Printed in the United States of America

To

Donna

Contents

vii

Acknowledgments

This book has long been in the making. The idea of translating two of the legal codes of the *leges barbarorum* occurred to me while attending doctoral seminars under the direction of Charles P. Loughran, S.J., of Fordham University. I owe it to the inspiration of Father Loughran that I was able to produce English translations of these two major legal sources of the early Middle Ages. I am also in debt to Loretta Denner for her helpful criticisms.

I also wish to express appreciation to the libraries of Fordham University, University of Rochester, Duke University, New York University, Columbia University, and the New York Public Library for making books available for this translation.

Theodore John Rivers
New York

Abbreviations

Beyerle Konrad Beyerle, ed. and trans. *Lex Baiuvariorum: Lichtdruck Wiedergabe der Ingolstädter Handschrift des bayerischen Volksrechts.* Munich, 1926.

Eckhardt A Karl August Eckhardt, ed. and trans. *Germanenrechte Texte und Übersetzungen,* Vol. 2, *Die Gesetze des Karolingerreiches.* Pt. 2, *Alemannen und Bayern.* Weimar, 1934.

Eckhardt B Karl August Eckhardt, ed. *Leges Alamannorum.* 1 and 2. Germanenrechte Neue Folge, Westgermanisches Recht, 6–7. Vol. 1: Göttingen, 1958. Vol. 2: Witzenhausen, 1962.

Lehmann Karl Lehmann, ed. *Leges Alamannorum. Monumenta Germaniae Historica,* Legum Sectio 1, Vol. 5, pt. 1. Rev. ed., Karl August Eckhardt. Hanover, 1966.

Schwind Ernst von Schwind, ed. *Lex Baiwariorum. Monumenta Germaniae Historica,* Legum Sectio 1, Vol. 5, pt. 2. Hanover, 1926.

Introduction

All peoples are governed by regulations. Whether these regulations are called laws or customs varies from culture to culture, but no people are without some prescribed way in which they regulate their society. Laws and customs may be defined as a person's rights to act in certain ways or a society's obligation to allow people to act in certain ways. The summation of these regulations, their application, and their enforcement constitute a legal system. The Germanic peoples who invaded and subsequently settled on territory occupied by the Roman Empire in the first six centuries of the Christian era possessed legal systems. Each of these Germanic peoples had its own laws, judicial system for the enforcement of the laws, and punishments for transgressions. Since the Germanic nations lived adjacent to one another, their laws are closely similar. Collectively, the Germanic laws form part of the *leges barbarorum,* that is, the Germanic or barbarian codes of law. All of the laws included in the barbarian codes of law were codified between the late fifth and the early ninth centuries.

The principal Germanic peoples who settled within the provinces of the Roman Empire were the Visigoths (Spain), the Franks and Burgundians (Gaul or France), and the Ostrogoths and Lombards (Italy). Other Germans settled in former Roman provinces—the Alamans and Bavarians (Switzerland and southern Germany) and the Angles and Saxons (England). All these Germanic nations promulgated laws, as the Frisians, Thuringians,

3

and continental Saxons, who settled in northern Germany and the Low Countries did in the early ninth century. The laws of all these Germans have survived. This is not true of other Germanic nations, such as the Vandals, who settled in northern Africa, or the Suevi, who settled in western Spain (Portugal). The Germans, those whose laws have survived and those whose laws have been lost, did not abandon their tribal ways when they came into contact with Roman culture; in fact, the Roman world influenced the Germans to put their oral laws into writing. The laws of two of the Germanic nations, the Alamans and Bavarians, are included in this book. Although there are modern German translations of the Alamannic and Bavarian legal codes, this is the first English translation. Before a description of the nature of Germanic law in general and Alamannic and Bavarian law in particular, a short history of the two nations follows.

HISTORY OF THE ALAMANS AND BAVARIANS

Alamans, 213–ca. 496 A.D.

Dio Cassius is the first Roman historian to describe the Alamans, placing them in the reign of Caracalla in 213 A.D. In that year, Caracalla led a successful campaign against them on the Main River. The Alamans, like many other Germans, had formed a confederation of several Germanic peoples, the Semnones, Juthungi, Bucinobantes, Lentienses, and Hermunduri, to render joint military aid to the individual members. The Alamans originally lived on the land bordering the Main River, but migrated to the upper Rhine, directly along the Rhine frontier, occupying the territory from the Rhine to the Danube. It was in this area, commonly called the Decuman Fields, that the Alamans were confederated. Alamans or Alamanni literally means "all the men," and in its original coinage probably meant "confederated men." They were well-armed and able fighters, and were especially noted for their horsemanship.

Approximately twenty years after Caracalla first encountered them, the Alamans began to plague the Romans by making inroads into Roman territory. The attacks began during the reign of the emperor Severus Alexander (222–35), who personally directed a campaign against them. In order to maintain peace, Severus Alexander was willing to pay subsidies to the Alamans, but his troops revolted, killed the emperor, and chose their commander, Maximin, as the new emperor (235). Maximin (235–

38) invaded Alamannia the same year and devastated the land. Peace ensued until the joint reigns of Valerian (253–58) and his son Gallienus (253–68). In 258, at the beginning of Gallienus' sole reign, the Alamans had invaded Rhaetia (Switzerland), destroyed Avenches, and penetrated into northern Italy. Having penetrated Italy as far as Milan, they were met there and defeated by Gallienus, but the Alamannic invasion of Rhaetia prevented complete recovery. The emperor strengthened Vindonissa (Windisch) in 260 and built additional forts to prevent other Alamannic invasions. The next emperor, Claudius Gothicus, crushingly defeated the Alamans in Rhaetia, but this did not prevent their leading a major invasion of Italy in 269. Aurelian (270–75) defeated them in 270 in two separate encounters. Shortly thereafter, in 274, Constantius Chlorus, general under Aurelian and father of Constantine I the Great, defeated the Alamans at Vindonissa.

The Franks and Alamans threatened the empire under Probus in 276–77. After defeating them, Probus required that they supply tribute to Rome. After 286, Diocletian and Maximian fought and subdued the Alamans, Franks, and Burgundians in Gaul. In 298, at Vindonissa, Constantius Chlorus defeated the Alamans, who had broken across the Rhine frontier and penetrated Gaul. Several thousand Alamans (the historical sources vary, giving numbers from 6,000 to 60,000) perished in battle in that year. Forts were built along the Rhine frontier in 298–99.

The closing of the third century saw peace between the Romans and the Alamans. Matters had not changed when Constantius' son, Constantine (306–37), continued his father's military career. In 306, when Constantine was declared augustus at York, one of his first duties was to secure the Rhine frontier against the Alamans and Franks. (Ironically, Constantine was declared augustus in England by Crocus, the Alamanic general who commanded Constantine's army.) Four years later, Constantine successfully turned away an attack of Alamans, Bructeri, Chamavi, and Cherusci. Later in his reign, in 328, Constantine directed a campaign against the Alamans at Trier on the Rhine frontier.

Gaul found itself without military defense when Magnentius, a usurper, moved his troops to the East to oppose Constantius (337–61). It was during this civil war that the Alamans under the leadership of Chnodomar invaded Gaul, burning several cities and ravaging its interior. Constantius moved westward after defeating Magnentius in 351, but was not successful against the Alamannic kings, notably Gundomad and Vadomar (354), nor against the Lentienses in 355. Constantius commissioned his relative Julian to subdue the Alamans in 356, and Julian proved to be more successful than Constantius. At the time Julian began his offensive against the Alamans, they held all of northeastern Gaul. He cleared it in two expeditions, the more famous of which culminated in the battle of Strasbourg (357). Of this battle, the Roman historian Ammianus Marcellinus records that 35,000 Alamannic warriors appeared, commanded by seven kings, one of whom was Chnodomar. Of these, 6,000 were slain, and several thousand more were drowned in the Rhine while fleeing the Romans. Julian pursued the fleeing Alamans into their own territory and soon after concluded peace with them (357). Some of the Alamans did not honor the truce and invaded Italy in 358, but peace was concluded again in 359. The Alamannic king Vadomar, against whom Constantius had not been successful in 354, penetrated into northern Italy in 360. He was arrested at a banquet given by Julian and deported, and Julian then attacked the Alamans. Julian left Gaul in 361 for the East to contest the rule of the empire with Constantius. The death of Constantius at Constantinople (361) led to Julian's being designated the next emperor (361–63). The removal of Julian's troops from the West in 361 left Gaul easy prey to future Germanic invasions.

Julian's successor, Valentinian I (363–75), spent nearly his entire reign in Gaul conducting campaigns against the Alamans and Franks. These expeditions were conducted from the emperor's residence at Trier, which sat directly on the Rhine frontier. While Valentinian was at Milan, Ursatius (his master of the offices) was rude to the Alamans who had been sent to greet the emperor on his accession. The Alamans retaliated by crossing the Rhine frontier and ravaging Gaul in 367, defeating a Roman army sent against them. Valentinian's forces, led by his commander of the cavalry, Jovinus, gave a crushing defeat to the Alamans at Châlons-sur-Marne (367). It was reported of the Alamannic casualties that 6,000 were killed and 4,000 wounded. The Romans suffered considerably lighter losses. In the following year, Valentinian crossed the Rhine frontier, invaded Alamannia, and routed the Alamans under King Rando. Valentinian began in 368 to strengthen existing forts and construct new ones along the entire length of the Rhine. Although Valentinian encouraged the

Burgundians to attack the Alamans in 370, the Burgundians declined to do so. The Romans led two more campaigns against the Alamans in 371 and 374. Peace was concluded between Valentinian and Macrianus, the Alamannic king, until the emperor left Gaul to defend the Danube frontier against the Quadi and Sarmatians, and Valentinian's son, Gratian (375–83), assumed the offensive against the Alamans. In 378, the Alamans assumed they would be met with little or no resistance because Gratian had gone to the East to lend aid to his uncle Valens. The Alamans took this opportunity and invaded Gaul. Gratian hastened back to Gaul and met the Alamans, notably the Lentienses, in the battle of Argentaria (near present-day Colmar) in 378. The Alamans were defeated. In the same year, Valens (364–78) had been killed in battle fighting the Goths at Adrianople. As a result of this German victory, the Danube frontier was permanently broken, allowing the Goths to penetrate the eastern provinces. Some headway was achieved against them, however, under Theodosius I (379–95), who marched against Eugenius, a puppet emperor raised to the purple by the Frank Arbogast. Theodosius fought Arbogast, his Franks, and Alamans on the banks of the river Frigidius, thirty-five miles from Aquileia in northern Italy (394), and defeated them. In the following year, the Roman Empire was permanently divided into halves, with Theodosius' son Honorius ruling in the West and his other son, Arcadius, ruling in the East.

It was during the reign of Honorius (395–423) that the Germans permanently broke through the Rhine frontier in the winter of 406–407, when Vandals, Suevi, Alans, Franks, Burgundians, and Alamans crossed the frozen Rhine. Some of these Germans attempted to establish kingdoms in northeastern Gaul in 411 when they proclaimed the Gaulish noble Jovinus emperor at Mainz. Ataulf the Visigoth, who regarded Jovinus as a threat to his own power and disputed his legitimacy, murdered Jovinus in 413. The Alamans settled along the Rhine frontier and in Rhaetia, the Franks and Burgundians settled in Gaul, while the Vandals, Suevi, and Alans (a non-Germanic people) passed through southern Gaul and into Spain, leading to the conquest and colonization of Spain (Suevi and Alans) and Africa (Vandals and Alans). Shortly thereafter the Visigoths also settled in Spain and southern Gaul, and the Ostrogoths in Italy. In 457, the Alamans penetrated into northern Italy but were successfully resisted by Emperor Majorian (457–61). In the 460s and 470s, there were other Alamannic incursions into Rhaetia and northern Italy, as a result of which Germanic kingdoms were established on Roman soil.

Marcomanni and Quadi (Bavarians), 58 B.C.–488 A.D.

The Bavarians are first described in Jordanes' *Getica* (*Origin and Deeds of the Goths*), which was written in 551. Although the Bavarians are believed to have made their first appearance about 500, they had been associated with the Roman Empire long before that date under different names. (The principal sources for this date are the *Getica* of Jordanes and the biography of St. Severin.) The Bavarians are essentially a confederation of Germanic tribes much like the Alamans, made up principally of the former Marcomanni and Quadi. The name Marcomanni is derived from the tribes living on the Roman frontier, meaning "men of the mark or border."

The earliest mention of the Marcomanni occurs in Caesar's *Gallic War,* in which they constitute a part of Ariovistus' Germanic army (58 B.C.). In the mid-first century B.C., the Marcomanni lived between the Main and Danube rivers. The first reference to the Quadi occurs in Strabo's *Geography* (completed ca. 27 A.D.), which places them in the Hercynian Forest, the heavily-forested mountains of Moravia.

Early in the first century A.D., the Marcomanni under King Maroboduus moved eastward, driving the Boii (a Celtic, not a Germanic, people) from Bohemia and settling in their place. The power of the Marcomanni at that time was considerable. The Marcomanni and their neighbors in Moravia, the Quadi, lived along the entire boundary of the Danube frontier. They therefore faced the Roman garrisons of Noricum and Vindelicia. In 6 A.D., Tiberius, then a general under Augustus, led a campaign against the Marcomanni in Bohemia, but the Romans had to sue for peace with Maroboduus because of an insurrection in Illyricum. The withdrawal of Roman forces allowed the Cherusci, another Germanic tribe, to attack the Marcomanni in 17 A.D., and Maroboduus' empire collapsed with the defeat of the Marcomanni in 19 A.D. Maroboduus asked to be allowed to enter Roman territory. Although granted this privilege, he was confined at Ravenna for the remainder of his life, dying in 35 A.D.

The next major confrontation between the Romans and the

Marcomanni and Quadi occurred during the Dacian war (85 A.D.), in which the empire under the Emperor Domitian (81–96 A.D.) suffered defeat. War also ensued between Domitian and these Germans in 89 A.D., terminating in the payment of annual tribute to the victorious Marcomanni.

The second century A.D. saw renewed campaigns against the Marcomanni and Quadi. In 167, they and other Germans invaded northern Italy, sacking it and eventually laying siege to Aquileia. This was the beginning of the Marcomannic war, which lasted until the death in 180 of the emperor, Marcus Aurelius, who led several campaigns against them. The Marcomanni were defeated in Pannonia and Noricum in 167–68. War was renewed in 169, but in 174 the Marcomanni were driven from Pannonia and severely defeated, and Pannonia was occupied by Roman troops. The Marcomanni and Quadi again took up hostilities in 177–78. Peace followed in the reign of Aurelius' son and successor, Commodus, and several thousand Quadi and Marcomanni were allowed to settle on Roman soil in agreement with the peace terms. There were renewed expeditions against these Germans in the first half of the third century, but the Romans were preoccupied with the Alamans at this time, regarding them as the greater threat.

In the third century, Philip the Arabian (243–49) led a notably successful campaign against the Quadi in 245–47. Later, in 254, the Marcomanni overran Pannonia and invaded Italy as far as Ravenna. The invasion in 254 occurred during the reign of Gallienus, who met and defeated the Marcomanni outside Milan, but he granted part of Pannonia to them on account of his marriage to the daughter of the Marcomannic king. Another invasion by the Quadi and Sarmatians (an Asiatic people, associated with the Alans) followed in 282. Warfare between the Marcomanni and the Romans was renewed in 296 and 297.

The beginning of the fourth century saw fighting between the empire and the Alamans, at a time when the Marcomanni and Quadi appear to have been fairly inactive. The mid-fourth century saw renewed encounters between the Roman Empire and several Germanic tribes. It was during Constantius' campaigns against the Alamans that his relative Julian led an offensive against the Quadi in 358. Later, in 364, while the Quadi and Sarmatians ravaged Pannonia the Alamans were laying waste to Rhaetia and Gaul. A decade later (373) the Quadi ravaged Pannonia and destroyed two Roman legions. Valentinian I responded by building forts on the left bank of the Danube, and the Quadi objected. The protest led to the murder of the Quadi king, Gabinius, and the Quadi along with the Sarmatians retaliated by devastating Moesia and Pannonia. In 375, Valentinian marched into Illyricum, which had been laid waste by the Quadi. He died from either a stroke or an epileptic seizure the same year, while receiving an embassy from the Quadi, who sought peace with the Romans.

In 405, the German Radagaisus led Ostrogoths, Vandals, Alans, and Quadi into Italy. They were defeated by Stilicho, Honorius' chief commander. In the winter of 406–407, the famous crossing of the frozen Rhine occurred. Whole tribes, including women and children, crossed with the intention of permanently settling in Gaul, and the Roman Empire was defenseless against their incursion. Although there still was a prefect of Noricum in 488, the Roman population in Vindelicia and Rhaetia began to emigrate to Italy. The Roman evacuation was followed by the settlement of the Marcomanni and Quadi. It was with this settlement that the name Bavarian appeared for the first time.

Alamans, 496–768 A.D.

The history of the Alamans from the end of the fifth century is closely linked with the history of the Merovingian Franks, though, technically, the duchy of Alamannia did not become a permanent part of Merovingian Gaul until 730. Although the Alamans and Franks pressured the Roman Empire over a long period of time, they also fought among themselves. There were, therefore, several wars between the Alamans and Franks before the famous battle in which the Salian Frankish King Clovis routed the Alamans at Tolbiac (Zülpich) in 496. In that year, the Alamans had attacked the Ripuarian Franks, and, since the latter feared defeat, they approached the Salian Franks for military assistance. Clovis (481–511) came to the rescue. Although it is generally believed that the Alamans were stronger than the Franks at the time of this battle, the Franks defeated them in Alsace, taking over their lands, which assumed the name of Franconia. Other Alamans fled southward into Baden, Württemberg, and Rhaetia, where they received the protection of Theodoric the Ostrogoth. The Alamans attempted to regain their independence in 503–504, but were defeated again by the Franks.

Southern Alamannia was under Ostrogothic control until Theodoric's death (526), while the original Alamannic lands in Alsace became part of the Frankish kingdoms. The defeat of the Alamans may be directly connected with the conversion of Clovis, since it was during the heat of battle that Clovis prayed to Christ to turn the battle in his favor, and vowed, if this occurred, to become a Christian. Up to this time, both the Franks and the Alamans were pagans. Nevertheless, the circumstances surrounding Clovis' conversion have recently been called into question, though whether we accept the true date of his conversion as 496 or 506, or the place of his baptism as Reims or Tours, does not preclude the fact that the Franks defeated the Alamans and subjected them to Frankish control. In any case, the conversion of Clovis aided the Franks in their territorial conquests, in which they received the support of the Church, enabling them to establish the strongest kingdom of the early Middle Ages.

Ten years after the death of Theodoric the Ostrogoth, all of Alamannia came under Frankish control. After this, there developed increased cooperation between Frank and Alaman during the Ostrogothic war (535–54). Most notable was the large army (reputed to have been 75,000 in number) of Alamans and Franks led by two Alamannic leaders, Leutharis and Buccelin, which marched into Italy for dubious reasons in 553, perhaps to take advantage of the worsening conditions there between the invading Byzantine army and the defending Ostrogoths. Although the Merovingian King Theodebald did not approve of the invasion, he appears to have made no effort to prevent it. The invaders were all but annihilated in 554, either by the plague or in battle.

At the beginning of the seventh century, the first redaction of the Alamannic laws (*Pactus legis Alamannorum*) was promulgated during the reign of Chlotar II (584–629), probably when he was sole king of Merovingian Gaul (613–29). From this time it may be said that Frankish rule over the Alamans was more than nominal. Other cooperation between Frank and Alaman occurred during the reign of Dagobert I (629–39); for example, in the latter's eastward drive against Samo and the Slavs (630), the Alamans were one of a group of Germans who fought for the Franks.

The Frankish influence in Alamannia (as well as in Bavaria) led to the conversion of the Alamans (and Bavarians) to Christianity. Irish missionaries entered Rhaetia in the late sixth and early seventh centuries. Most notable was St. Columbanus, who preached to the Alamans at Lake Constance about 610. The conversion of the Alamans was part of a monastic movement that spread from the monastery of Luxeuil, itself recently founded (590) in southeastern Gaul. St. Columbanus left behind his pupil Gallus, who founded a monastery (later named after him, that is, the monastery of St. Gall), which became one of the greatest learning centers in western Europe. Although St. Columbanus introduced the Celtic, rather than the Roman, rule among the Alamans, Alamannic foundations were reorganized in the 740s under the Benedictine (that is, Roman) rule. Other Alamannic monasteries were Reichenau (724) and Rheinau (731).

Alamannia was formally independent until 730, at which time the Merovingian mayor of the palace, Charles Martel, terminated Alamannic independence and reduced Alamannia from an autonomous duchy to a dependent province—although, as was said above, the loss of independence had its roots as far back as the defeat of the Alamans by Clovis. The histories of the Alamans and the Franks were closely associated for several reasons: the Alamans lived directly to the east of Merovingian Gaul and were seen as a constant threat, a situation that led to repeated military campaigns by the Franks against the Alamans to bring them under Frankish control; furthermore, Alamannic vassals had served in the Merovingian armies and thereby gradually lost their independence; the Alamans were Christianized and lost the paganism that had unified them against the Franks; and, significantly, the Alamannic laws were promulgated under direct supervision of Frankish law (especially the *Lex Salica*) and administration.

The loss of Alamannic independence in the eighth century may be briefly summarized. In the early years of the eighth century the Alamans under Duke Godefrid proclaimed their independence from the Franks. The Merovingian mayor of the palace at this time was Pepin II of Heristal, who led several campaigns against the Alamans between 709–12 and reduced them again to Merovingian authority. The desire for independence led to uprisings under Duke Lantfrid (712–30) under whose direction the final redaction of the Alamannic laws (*Lex Alamannorum*) was promulgated. Pepin II's son, Charles Martel (714–41), undertook several expeditions against the Alamans in 720, 722, and 724. In 730, Charles Martel reduced Alamannia to a Merovingian province, although not all resistance was broken. After Charles Martel died in 741, the Alamans revolted, along with other subject peoples, such as the Bavarians, Saxons, and Frisians. In 742, Charles' sons, Pepin III and Carloman, invaded Alamannia, and there were other expeditions in 744 and 745. One of the final acts of violence occurred in 746, when several principal Alamannic leaders were summoned by Carloman to an assembly at Cannstadt and murdered. (Carloman appears to have had remorse for his action, because in the following year he resigned his power to his brother Pepin and entered a monastery. He died in the monastery of Monte Cassino in 754.) Alamannia became one of the provinces of the Franks. On the death of Pepin III in 768, Alamannia was given to his son Carloman along with Burgundy and Aquitaine, while his other son, Charles (Charlemagne, 768–814), received Austrasia and most of Neustria.

Bavarians, 488–794 A.D.

Like Alamannia, Bavaria lost its independence to the Franks in the eighth century, though this came about differently. Bavaria maintained its autonomy longer because of its greater distance from the Franks, yet lost it in several stages. As was said above, the Bavarians were essentially a confederation of tribes, especially the Marcomanni and Quadi, who made their first appearance about 500 A.D. The movement of the Bavarians from Bohemia to Pannonia (Roman Noricum broke down in 488) is believed to have occurred simultaneously with the movement of the Lombards, who invaded and permanently settled in Italy beginning in 568, after the fall of the Ostrogothic kingdom (554) and the temporary restoration of Roman (that is, Byzantine) rule. There were close ties between the Bavarians and the Lombards until the fall of Bavaria to Charlemagne in 788.

Theudebert (534–48), the Merovingian king, attempted to expand Frankish power into Italy and southern Germany. This brought him into direct confrontation with the Bavarians, whom he also wished to subdue. He succeeded in doing this about 543. Shortly thereafter, the first Bavarian duke was created in the person of Garibald (ca. 555–95), who was the first duke from the ruling family of the Agilolfingi. The hopes of the subject Bavarians must have been raised with the creation of this ducal office. Garibald extended Bavarian influence by allowing his Catholic daughter, Theodelinda, to marry the Arian Lombard

King Authari in 589, and upon Authari's death (590), she married the next Lombard king, Agilulf. The Franks viewed these marriages as a threat, and as a result the Frankish King Childebert (575–96) invaded Bavaria. Childebert was forced to retreat because of a revolt within his own kingdom, but not before he had dethroned Garibald and installed his relative (Garibald and the Merovingian king were related, since Garibald had married into the Merovingian family). In 574, Bavarians were included in Sigebert's army, which he sent against Chilperic. Dagobert I appealed to the Bavarians for military aid in 630, when he demanded restitution from Samo the Slav, who had killed several Frankish merchants in Samo's kingdom. The Bavarians, however, had been fighting the Slavs (Wends) in their own right since 593.

The latter half of the seventh century saw the Bavarians obtaining more and more freedom from the Franks until they became virtually independent under the leadership of Duke Theodo II. Frankish pressure was again applied to Bavaria under Charles Martel, who defeated the Bavarians in 725. Charles Martel also took over the duchy of Alamannia in 730 and appointed no successor to the last duke, Lantfrid, who died in 730. The religious reorganization of the Bavarian church (discussed below) served as another tie binding Frank and Bavarian. Both the Alamans and the Bavarians rose in revolt after the death of Charles Martel (741), but were defeated by Charles's sons, Pepin III and Carloman. The Bavarians and their Duke Odilo (731–48) were defeated by the Franks on the banks of the river Lech in 743. Odilo, like many other Bavarian dukes before him, was related to the Franks (he married the daughter of Charles Martel, Childtrudis); he had also supported the reorganization of the Bavarian church spearheaded by St. Boniface.

The conversion of Bavaria itself commenced with the invitation given by Duke Theodo II to St. Rupert (Hrodbert), which led to St. Rupert's founding a monastery for men and a convent for women at Salzburg (696). He is remembered as the apostle to the Bavarians. Shortly thereafter, St. Corbinian founded a monastery at Freising (724); the monasteries of Regensburg (732) and Passau (738) followed. Despite these advances, the Bavarian church lacked discipline. It was in this context that Pope Gregory III made St. Boniface papal vicar for all Germany in 738 to restore and reorganize the Bavarian church. Boniface also received the support of Duke Odilo, who saw the need for reform. Boniface purged the church of schism, held synods, reintroduced monastic discipline, and adopted canon law in accordance with Rome. Diocesan organization of Bavaria was introduced by Boniface (739) and administered by the creation of four bishoprics, one each at Salzburg, Freising, Regensburg, and Passau. In 741, a fifth bishopric was founded, at Eichstätt. The bishopric of Würzburg followed in 742. There were important church councils in Bavaria during these formative years, the councils of Aschheim (756), Dingolfing (770), and Neuching (772).

The years which followed the death of Odilo (d. 748) were the beginning of the end for an independent Bavaria. Although the reign of the last duke (Tassilo III, 748–88, son of Duke Odilo and Childtrudis, daughter of Charles Martel) lasted four decades, it was characterized by increased submission to foreign intervention. (The *Lex Baiuvariorum* was promulgated at this time, between 744 and 748.) The first sign of the loss of independence occurred in 757, when the young Duke Tassilo had to commend himself to his uncle Pepin III at an assembly at Compiègne. This is the first recorded act of commendation, in which a vassal, Tassilo, placed his clasped hands between those of his lord. As Pepin's vassal, Tassilo was obliged to furnish Pepin with military service, which he refused to do at the assembly at Nevers (763), during Pepin's Aquitanian campaign.

Tassilo further jeopardized his people's independence by pursuing a pro-Lombard policy, aided by his marriage to Liutberga, a daughter of the Lombard king, Desiderius. The marriage was not well received by Charlemagne (768–814), who had married another daughter of Desiderius, but had repudiated her shortly thereafter for unknown reasons. In 772, Tassilo sent his son, Theodo, to Rome to be baptized by the pope, at the very time when Desiderius, his father-in-law, was at war with the papacy. The overthrow of the Lombard kingdom in 774 by Charlemagne worked to Tassilo's disadvantage. Pro-Frankish sympathies were evolving in Bavaria, nurtured by various nobles and by Bishop Arbeo of Freising. Tassilo sent Bavarians to Charlemagne's Spanish expedition in 778 and renewed his oath of fealty to Charlemagne at Worms in 781. The conflict came to a head in 787, when Charlemagne summoned Tassilo to appear at Worms and Tassilo refused. Charlemagne prepared to invade Bavaria, and Tassilo capitulated. He surrendered the duchy and received it back as a benefice, and took the oath of vassalage again to Charlemagne. However, Tassilo's wife, Liutberga persuaded him in 787 to rebel, and he formed an alliance with the pagan Avars who lived just east of Bavaria. A number of his nobles deserted him, and he was forced to appear before Charlemagne in 788 at the assembly of Ingelheim. Tassilo was accused of the capital offense of desertion (*herisliz*) and was condemned to death at this assembly, but his life was spared. Tassilo was tonsured and forced to become a monk at Jumièges, and his wife and children also were forced to take up the monastic life. Bavaria was subdued and annexed to Charlemagne's vast empire, and the long line of dukes terminated. Bavaria was governed by a relative of Charlemagne's, Duke Gerold, and under him, by a group of Frankish counts. At the council of Frankfurt (794), Tassilo was again forced to renounce all claim to his duchy, and Bavaria became part of the Carolingian empire.

GERMANIC LAW

Primitive law, of which Germanic law forms a part, is largely taken up with the idea of custom. Compared to the scope of modern law, custom appears to be uncertain in its form and equally indefinite in its application, but, quite to the contrary, it made a primitive society rigid in many respects. The regulations of a primitive world were more fixed because they were cloaked with the idea of sanction. All custom become more or less sacred; its violation brought a person into direct confrontation with punishment, and punishment was rigidly applied to make the offender conform to the accepted norm. As a result, transgressions were punished more quickly in a more primitive society than in a less primitive one. Spontaneity of punishment and civic responsibility are two of the basic characteristics of primitive law. There are numerous primitive societies whose development parallels that of Germanic society, including American Indian, African, Near Eastern (Hittite, Assyrian, etc.), Celtic, Scandinavian, Hindu, and Chinese societies.

Originally, Germanic law was custom, that is, a body of traditions handed down orally from one generation to another. New laws, theoretically, could not be made in this early period of the Germanic migrations. The ultimate authority in this legal system was the king, whose chief legal function was to speak the law—

to decide legal cases by enforcing exactly what the law said; he could not make new law. The Germanic contact with Roman civilization induced the Germans to put their oral customs into writing, and Germanic tribalism lost some of its simplicity when custom became customary law. The importance of the king in the Germanic legal system increased with the development of customary law, once the Germans came under direct influence of Roman institutions.

The extent of Roman legal influence on Germanic custom varied. In those areas where Roman culture was the strongest, that is, in southern Europe, Roman influence on Germanic custom was strongest; in northern Europe, where Roman culture was weaker, Germanic custom was less strongly influenced. In addition, those Germanic nations which had longest contact with the Romans experienced the greatest amount of influence, so that the laws of the Visigoths and Ostrogoths show the greatest Roman legal influence, while the laws of the Frisians, Thuringians, and continental Saxons show the least. Roman legal influence on Germanic custom was based not so much on the technicalities of Roman law, but on the fact that it was written. Like many other primitive societies, the Germans kept no written records, which is why the earliest history of the Germans is known only through the writings of Romans, such as Caesar (first century B.C.) and Tacitus (late first and early second century A.D.).

Under the Germanic legal system, disputes between Germans were settled by Germanic law. Disputes between two Romans under Germanic rule were settled by Roman law, although only in so far as a particular Germanic nation had promulgated a law for its Roman subjects; the Romans supervised the promulgation of Roman law by the Germans, since the Germans themselves were largely ignorant of Roman law. However, disputes between a German and a Roman were settled by the law of the conqueror, that is, by Germanic law. (An exception to this was Ostrogothic law, in which disputes between an Ostrogoth and a Roman were settled by Roman law.) An important difference between the Germanic and Roman legal systems is that Roman law was characterized by territoriality, and Germanic law by personality. According to the principle of territoriality, any person living within a geographically-defined area, regardless of that person's national origin, was subject to the law of the land. Personality of law was characterized by the law under which a person was born, and which he carried with him, wherever he traveled. In a case, for example, between a Lombard and a Bavarian in which the Bavarian was the defendant, the Bavarian had the right to be tried according to his own law, and not Lombard law, even if the crime took place outside Bavaria. Yet, the principles of territoriality and personality existed simultaneously on different levels for the Germanic nations. Once the Germanic kingdoms were firmly settled in western Europe, their personal laws assumed some properties of territorial law. Foreigners, for example, were given protection by the king and were allowed this protection wherever they traveled within a foreign nation, yet personality was still applied in the conflict of laws and in private law. Territoriality of law began to predominate again in the ninth century.[1]

At the time the Germans were writing their laws down, Roman law was undergoing transformations. Because the Germans represented a different and simpler culture than the Romans, and because they had conquered the Roman provinces, they had little understanding of or use for the technicalities of classical Roman law. Roman law was applied only among Romans, but because of the general decline of Roman culture in the early Middle Ages, Roman legal institutions also suffered, though the Romans constituted the majority of the population. This resulted, as far as law was concerned, in the degeneration of Roman classical law into a form called Roman vulgar law. The simpler version of Roman law applied in western Europe is called West Roman vulgar law, and included laws promulgated under the direction of the Visigoths, Burgundians, and Ostrogoths. These laws are, respectively, the *Lex Romana Visigothorum,* the *Lex Romana Burgundionum,* and the *Edictum Theoderici.*[2] An example of a Germanic nation that had Roman subjects but did not promulgate a Roman law was the kingdom of the Franks, and, in this case, Romans living under Frankish rule were subject to Frankish (either Salic or Ripuarian) law.

Besides the Alamannic and Bavarian laws translated in this book, the principal Germanic laws are the *Lex Salica, Lex Ribuaria, Lex Burgundionum, Lex Romana Burgundionum, Leges Visigothorum, Lex Romana Visigothorum, Edictum Theoderici, Leges Langobardorum,* and Anglo-Saxon law. (The *Lex Frisionum, Lex Saxonum,* and *Lex Thuringorum* were issued early in the ninth century under the direction of Charlemagne, as were the bulk of the capitularies, but none of these laws will be described in this brief introduction.) The oldest of the laws is the first edition of the *Leges Visigothorum,* known as the *Codex Euricianus* (476). All of the laws were written in Latin, with the exception of Anglo-Saxon law, which was written in West Saxon (Old English).

One of the most well-known Germanic laws is the *Lex Salica* (Salic Law), often attributed to Clovis (481–511). Unfortunately, like many other Germanic laws, the Salic Law contains no date to pinpoint it accurately, and to this predicament are added textual problems. One of the principal difficulties in interpreting the Salic Law is selecting the most accurate text, since there are manuscripts which contain 65, 80, and 100 legal titles each. The 65-title text is the oldest of the three, and the 100-title text the most recent. The problems of the *Lex Salica* are complicated further by the survival of an early form of the *Lex Salica,* known as the *Pactus legis Salicae.* Chapters of the *Lex Salica* are believed to have been promulgated at different times, combining both ancient Germanic custom and recent legislation. The law was originally pagan with no Christian influence, but Christian laws were introduced under the influence of the *Pactum pro tenore pacis* of Childebert I and Chlotar I (511–58) and the *Edictum Chilperici* (561–84). Charlemagne (768–814) further modified the *Lex Salica* by correcting its crude Latin, eliminating unintelligible laws, and adding new ones. The *Lex Salica* is primarily a penal law, and is concerned with the redress of crimes (murder, theft, mutilation, exploitation of women) by monetary means.

The *Lex Ribuaria* (Ripuarian Law), which is partly based on the *Lex Salica,* represents the custom of the Ripuarian Franks, a Germanic nation closely related to the Salian Franks. Most of the *Lex Ribuaria* is believed to have been promulgated after 596 (that is, after the date of the *decretio* of Childebert II). Other parts of these laws may have been promulgated by Dagobert I (629–39). Of the 89 titles in the *Lex Ribuaria,* titles 1–38 indicate the influence of the Salic Law, but require slightly higher monetary compensation; titles 39–54 are taken verbatim from the *Lex Salica;* and titles 55–89 may have been added considerably later, perhaps during the early Carolingian period. Much like the *Lex Salica,* the *Lex Ribuaria* is primarily a penal code, indicating little non-Germanic influence, although Christian influence is evident.

The laws that pertained to the Burgundian people were the *Lex Burgundionum* (*Liber Constitutionum*), promulgated in part by Gundobad between the years 483–516, by his son Sigimund after 517, and by Godomar III between the years 524–32. These Burgundian laws applied to the Burgundians, while the *Lex Romana Burgundionum* pertained to the Roman population living under Burgundian rule. The Burgundian laws include later additions, known as the *Constitutiones extravagantes,* issued during the reign of Godomar.

The *Lex Romana Burgundionum* (ca. 500 A.D.) was promulgated by Gundobad for the use of Roman citizens living in the Burgundian kingdom. These laws are based on Roman legislation: the *Codex Gregorianus,* the *Codex Hermogenianus,* the *Codex Theodosianus,* post-Theodosian constitutions, and the writings of two Roman jurists, Gaius' *Institutes* and Paul's *Sentences.* Yet these laws were short-lived, since the *Lex Romana Visigothorum* was used in place of the *Lex Romana Burgundionum* when the Burgundians were defeated by the Merovingian Franks in 534 and Burgundy was annexed to Merovingian Gaul.

Like the Burgundians, the Visigoths promulgated different laws for themselves and their Roman subjects. The earliest edition of Visigothic law, the *Codex Euricianus,* appeared under King Euric in 476. Unfortunately, the bulk of its 350 laws are lost, although laws numbered 276 to 336 have survived, and some of these were used as the basis of corresponding Bavarian laws. Euric's code also shows some Roman influence. King Leovigild (568–86) revised Euric's laws by adding new laws (known as the *Codex revisus*), but he issued laws only for the Visigothic population in Spain. Chindaswinth revised Leovigild's laws, and this revision was continued by his son, Recceswinth (649–72). Recceswinth, more than any other Visigothic king, is credited with promulgating the *Leges Visigothorum.* This body of law contains 324 of Leovigild's revised laws (known as the *Antiquae*), 99 laws of Chindaswinth, and 87 laws of Recceswinth. A few laws of minor Visigothic kings were also included. These laws comprised the *Leges Visigothorum* (654), which replaced the *Lex Romana Visigothorum.* The Visigothic laws as promulgated by Recceswinth applied to both Gothic and Hispano-Roman subjects in Spain. The *Leges Visigothorum* are subdivided into twelve sections, devoted mostly to matters of procedural law, marriage, theft, general violence, kinship disputes, land law, business enterprises, and flight from justice, among others. These laws were revised by Erwig in 681 as the *Lex Visigothorum renovata,* some of which were later repealed by Egica (687–702).

The *Lex Romana Visigothorum* was promulgated by the Visigothic king, Alaric II, in 506, and is based on the same sources as the *Lex Romana Burgundionum.* The *Lex Romana Visigothorum,* which is also known as the *Breviarium Alaricianum* (*Breviary of Alaric*), may have been promulgated to gain the support of the Catholic Gallo-Roman population living under Visigothic sovereignty in southwestern Gaul (the Visigoths were Arian). *Interpretationes* (commentaries) were added to the Roman sources used in these laws, containing summaries or paraphrases of the sources of Roman law. The *Lex Romana Visigothorum* was the standard text of Roman law in the Middle Ages before the reintroduction of classical Roman law in the twelfth century in the form of Justinian's *Corpus Juris Civilis.*

The *Edict of Theoderic* (*Edictum Theoderici*) was issued by Theoderic the Ostrogoth for disputes that arose between Ostrogoths and Romans in Italy; otherwise, disputes among Romans only were settled by Roman law, and disputes among Ostrogoths, by Ostrogothic law. This edict contained predominantly Roman law, to which was added Ostrogothic law, but the two legal systems, the Germanic and the Roman, were not closely integrated. The edict, issued between 493 and 507, contains 154 laws, divided into private, criminal, and procedural law. The Roman legal sources in the edict are the three Roman law codes (*Gregorianus, Hermogenianus,* and *Theodosianus*), some post-Theodosian constitutions, and Paul's *Sentences.* Of the three West Roman vulgar laws, Ostrogothic, Burgundian, and Visigothic (all of which are indicative of the degeneration of classical Roman law in Western Europe), the *Edictum Theoderici* is by far the simplest.

The Lombard laws (*Leges Langobardorum*) were the personal laws of the Lombards, who invaded Italy in 568. The Lombard laws applied only to northern and central Italy; southern Italy never came under Lombard control. The first king to promulgate a legal code of unwritten Lombard custom was Rothair, and the promulgation was known as *Rothair's Edict* (*Edictum Rothari*), issued in 643. *Rothair's Edict,* containing 388 laws, constituted the basis of the Lombard laws, which later laws either supplemented or modified. Later additions to *Rothair's Edict* were the nine laws by Grimwald (668), the 153 laws of Liutprand

(713–35), the fourteen laws of Ratchis (745 or 746), and the twenty-four laws of Aistulf (750 and 755). The 588 laws of the five kings constitute what one traditionally calls the Lombard laws, that is, the laws issued by the Lombards while they maintained their independence. After the subjugation of the Lombards to Charlemagne in 774, the Carolingian capitularies issued for the Lombards beginning in 776, and the laws issued in reaction to Carolingian sovereignty by Aregis in 774 and Adelchis in 866 are merely supplemental. Lombard legislation for all practical purposes had ceased by 774.

The Angles and Saxons in England, like the continental Germans, promulgated laws (dooms), but these were written in West Saxon (Old English), and not in Latin. The first to appear were the laws of Aethelberht of Kent (dated between 565 and 604), which contain pure Germanic custom and show no sign of Roman influence. Laws of two other Kentish legislators followed, those of Hlothere and Eadric (685–86) and Wihtred (695). Simultaneous with Wihtred's laws were Ine's (688–95), the first laws promulgated by a West Saxon king, and these were followed by the laws of Alfred (890–99). Alfred attempted to produce laws that would be universal throughout England, preserving the best laws from the past and adding new laws of his own. Some Anglo-Saxon laws, such as those of Earconberht of Kent (640–64) or Offa of Mercia (757–96) have been lost. Alfred's laws were followed by, among others, laws of Edward the Elder (901–25), Aethelstan (925–40), Edmund (942–46), and Edgar (946–63). Aethelred produced a great deal of legislation near the end of the Anglo-Saxon period between 991 and 1016, which Cnut (Canute) completed in a two-part code of laws (1027–34), the first half of which are ecclesiastical laws and the latter half secular. Anglo-Saxon laws had an influence beyond the Anglo-Saxon period, since they influenced the legal development of the Anglo-Norman period.

The individual Germanic law codes briefly described above do not contain all the laws of the Germanic nations. There were laws that there was no need to reinforce with a written law, either because the laws were infrequently applied or because they were uncontroversial. What has survived in the *leges barbarorum* are laws which needed clarification, or in some cases, new laws replacing obsolete ones. The vast majority of barbarian laws concern the disposition of crimes; they offer little in the way of laws that deal with anything other than redressing personal rights. The principal crimes described in the Germanic laws, as well as in the Alamannic and Bavarian laws, are murder, assault, theft (including selling into slavery), treason, arson, rape, adultery and related sexual offenses, among others. A number of the crimes named deal with various types of physical injury, and these are described in the greatest detail, even in so far as specifying which joint of which finger was injured. Most Germanic laws concern private law, that is, conflicts between individuals.

Crimes among the Germans at the time of their written laws were settled by monetary payment. This recompense legally satisfied the family or clan whose member was victimized through some criminal act. If the injured party or his family refused the payment, a blood feud might result. Social pressure was applied, however, to assure that monetary payment would be accepted and peace reestablished. Fear of the feud encouraged settlement, since any member of the criminal's kin could be singled out to receive the vendetta from the victim's kin. There was also the chance that victim and criminal were related, forcing both parties to come to a settlement. The underlying principle of the feud was revenge, by virtue of which the victim (or his kin) not only punished those who violated his rights but also defended his personal honor and removed the stigma of shame from himself and his kin. Personal injuries ranged from striking another with a fist or cutting off another's finger to taking another's life. Recompense was also given for injury to property.

As in other primitive societies, kin (persons related by blood) played an important role in the everyday life of Germanic society. Kinship was the basis of social organization and interpersonal cooperation. Such concepts as legal rights and duties, marriage, and laws of inheritance found meaning through one's kin. For example, the kin were expected to help a relative in the monetary payment for a crime, with the nearest kin paying most and the most distant least. Among the Saxons in England, the patrilateral kin received more if a relative was victimized through some criminal act than the victim's matrilateral kin. Since Germanic society was patriarchal, Germans traced their descent through their father's ancestors, not through their mother's. Closely connected with the idea of kin were the principles of personal freedom and value of the spoken word. Although these will be discussed below, suffice it to say here that unless a person had kin he could not legally defend himself before his peers and was very nearly isolated from society.

ALAMANNIC AND BAVARIAN LEGAL CODES

The two Germanic codes of law contained in this translation, namely, the Alamannic laws (*Lex Alamannorum*) and Bavarian laws (*Lex Baiuvariorum*), are part of the corpus of the *leges barbarorum*. Although both laws were promulgated in the mid-eighth century, which places them later in time than many other Germanic laws, they are still characteristic of Germanic institutions before western Europe became substantially feudal. Western Europe under feudalism was characterized by its own system of social organization, distinct from, though based in part upon, Germanic customs. There are also a number of Germanic terms that supplement the meaning of the original Latin in these codes, including the Alamannic and Bavarian laws, and these terms greatly aid in the study of Germanic tribal customs.

The laws that are collectively called the Alamannic laws actually constitute a second legal code, since the first and more primitive Alamannic laws have also survived and are known as the *Pactus legis Alamannorum*. (The Salic Law, *Lex Salica,* also has an earlier form, known as the *Pactus legis Salicae.*) The *Pactus legis Alamannorum* is thought to have appeared about 613; the Alamannic laws, which are a later compilation, appeared about 717–19; and the Bavarian laws about 744–48. Neither the Alamannic and Bavarian laws nor the *Pactus* can be pinpointed to a definite year, since they lack dates; yet because they refer to persons and events whose dates can be determined with a marked degree of accuracy, supplemented by other historical sources, the dates given above contain only a small margin of error.[3]

The laws of the Alamans and Bavarians may be classified into three divisions: ecclesiastical, public (ducal), and private law. Respectively, these are laws with the following titles: *L. Alam.* I–XXII and *L. Baiu.* I; *L. Alam.* XXIII–XLIII and *L. Baiu.* II–III; and *L. Alam.* XLIV–XCVIII and *L. Baiu.* IV–XXIII [XXII]. Under each title are numerous individual laws, more in one category (private) than in another (public and ecclesiastical). Both the Alamannic and Bavarian laws have the same three divisions in the same order, showing a fairly strong degree of similarity. This similarity is enhanced by a critical evaluation of the contents of individual laws and by their philological similarities; there are even verbatim laws found in both codes. All this indicates that the earlier of these laws (Alamannic) was consulted when the later (Bavarian) was promulgated; both appeared within twenty years of each other.[4] Since the Alamannic and Bavarian laws strongly resemble the laws of the Merovingian Franks, it may be assumed that the Franks played a dominant role in the promulgation of the law codes. In fact, the prologue of the Bavarian code explicitly states that the laws of the Alamans, Bavarians, and Franks were promulgated under Theuderic I (511–34), the Merovingian king, who chose men learned in the law to make old pagan custom conform to Christian law. The Bavarian laws, like the Alamannic, may be a later compilation, based in part upon an earlier form similar to the *Pactus legis Alamannorum*.

The Germanic laws concerned more than personal injuries; they also concerned compensation for taking another's life. Injury to another's property as well as injury to his person constituted monetary indebtedness. Taking another's life was a far more serious crime, and this was compensated with payment of the *wergeld,* the total monetary value of a person's life, to prevent the blood feud. Since Germanic society was a class society, people from a higher class had a higher wergeld, since their total value was greater. In Alamannic and Bavarian societies, a freeman's life was worth 160 solidi (see the discussion below on the *solidus*), a freedman's life was valued at forty solidi, while a slave's was placed at twenty solidi. Payment of the wergeld could be made in any form, in coin, livestock, land, or other valuable property. Additional payments could be exacted, besides the simple monetary payment or the wergeld. This additional payment was the *fredus,* the payment rendered into the public treasury in compensation for the breaking of the public peace, whose guardian was the duke or king. For the Alamans and Bavarians, this meant that the duke received a fee for particular crimes. Not all crimes were protected by wergeld or monetary compensation and a *fredus;* only those offenses in which someone took unfair advantage of another or endangered a church or the ducal office received both. The double penalty might be exacted for forcibly removing a fugitive from a church after he sought sanctuary there, killing someone in a church, injuring the clergy, stealing property from a church or the duke, knowingly buying stolen property, pledging property illegally, or neglecting to come to the tribal assembly once summoned to appear.

In Alamannic and Bavarian societies, the idea of personal freedom was closely intertwined with class. There were three principal classes, slave, freed, and free, though the barriers between them were not fixed. It was possible to lose one's freedom or regain it, although the former was easier than the latter. The difference in class, therefore, expresses the difference in social condition. Slaves were those who had lost their freedom; freedmen were those who had regained their freedom; and freemen were those who never lost their freedom. Slavery in the early Middle Ages had survived from the Roman Empire. Although the Church helped to improve the slave's conditions by giving him protection, it also perpetuated slavery well into the medieval period. Slaves were not free agents; they had no rights and were outside the law's protection. Slaves who committed crimes were punished corporeally, or their masters paid the monetary compensation, or both. Only slaves were whipped, blinded, or had their hands cut off. Such severe punishments were rarely applied to the other classes, unless the duke or the society was threatened. Since slaves had no legal freedom and no rights, their total value, that is, their wergeld, was less than that of freedmen and freemen. A slave's wergeld was less because his total worth was considered less, although he might have been a freeman before becoming a slave. The class of freemen itself was subdivided according to wealth and was headed by the duke and his immediate family. Because freemen had a higher wergeld than the classes below them and were better able to pay compensation, the upper classes were definitely favored at the expense of the poor. It was easier for a wealthy person to violate the law, pay a fine, and keep his freedom than for a poorer person.

Some of the names of the people to be found within the three principal classes follow. A male slave was called simply *servus;* a female slave was called *ancilla* (maidservant). There was also the *mancipium,* a slave who worked on a seigneurie or manor, an agricultural estate. Directly above the slaves were freedmen, called *frilaz* in the Bavarian laws. Although now freed, the *frilaz* did not have equal rights with freemen, since they had been stigmatized at one time with the lack of freedom or legal rights. There were various levels of free classes. A member of one of the lower free classes was the *colonus,* who, like the *mancipium,* was indentured on a manor. The *coloni* evolved into the serfs of the Middle Ages. The *colonus,* who was a freeman, and the *mancipium* and *servus,* who were slaves, were all required to render service (*servitium*) and tribute (*tributum*) to the lay or ecclesiastical lord on whose land they worked. The agricultural conditions set down in the Alamannic and Bavarian laws closely approximate the conditions of the later medieval manor. Concerning the land-owning classes, all of whom were free, the Alamannic laws mention the *minoflidus,* which represented the lower free landowning class. This class was directly above the *colonus.* In addition, there were at least two classes above the *minoflidus.* These were the next two free classes, called, in Latin, the middle (*medianus*) and the upper (*primus*) classes. The wergelds of all these classes were different: for the *minoflidus* (ordinary freeman) the wergeld was 160 solidi, for the *medianus,* 200 solidi, and for the *primus,* 240 solidi.

A freeman in Germanic society could lose his freedom in a number of ways: if he was unable to pay the compensation for a crime, if he was captured in war, if he was sold into slavery through abduction, if he committed incest, if he committed treason, or if he refused to cease working on Sunday after being repeatedly warned; he could also marry into slavery. A slave (by birth or otherwise) in Germanic society could be freed in several ways, but manumission by a charter in a church became the most common method. There were other forms of manumission; in Lombard society, for example, a slave was freed in a ceremony at the crossroads, and among the Merovingian Franks, a denarius (silver penny) was tossed in the presence of the king, signifying that the slave's master had terminated his need for the slave. Other methods are poorly understood, such as manumission by relatives while the slave served in the army. Manumitting a slave in a church became the acceptable manner. It not only gave the slave's master encouragement that he might profit from this deed spiritually, but, since any local church would do, it was a far more convenient method than manumission at the crossroads or the King's court. More importantly, the slave's freedom was validated in writing through a charter. Since the charter was written in a largely illiterate age, only the clergy could write the charter and read its contents; the manumission ceremony, therefore, enhanced the authority of the church. There are references to this form of manumission in the Alamannic laws.

Once freed, however, a former slave was not viewed by his society as totally liberated. Although a freedman had more rights than a slave, he did not attain the full status of a freeman. A freedman was ultimately dependent on the king or duke, since if the freedman died leaving no heirs, his property was confiscated by the government. A manumitted woman who married a slave after she received her freedom lost it again. Free Alamannic women who married into slavery and performed their work had the option of being freed by their relatives within three years, but after this period they could not be freed, and remained slaves for the rest of their lives. Children born into this marriage were born slaves. Furthermore, a freedman's wergeld was less than a freeman's. Since a recently-liberated slave did not have the financial means to maintain his freedom if he committed a major crime, he could easily lapse back into servitude. Nevertheless, manumissions may have been quite common. Given the simple agricultural life in a society concerned primarily with day-to-day survival, the status of a freedman differed little from that of a slave, and both of these differed little from the free *colonus*. All of them had to work for a landowner as indentured tenants.

Status, then, was defined, though not rigid. Because Germanic society was a class society, individuals carried their status with them, just as they carried their personal tribal law with them. The status of a slave was the lowest, since, as was said above, he had no rights and was under the complete jurisdiction of his master. The status of the duke was the highest, since there was no individual whose authority exceeded his. Yet, ultimately, even the dukes were forced to recognize the supremacy of the Merovingian and Carolingian Franks. The vast majority of the people in Alamannic and Bavarian societies, as in early medieval society, were peasants. It was possible for them to improve their status by marrying into a class above their own. Likewise, status could be lowered by marrying into a lower class. Personal status ultimately became linked to economic condition. Explicit references are found in the Alamannic and Bavarian laws to improving and lessening individual status.

The family was clearly important in Germanic society. It was the family that protected the individual and supported him in the blood feud, and people without blood relatives were at the mercy of the law if they incurred a legal debt greater than they could pay. The family received the *wergeld* if one of its members was killed. At the time the Alamannic and Bavarian laws were promulgated, the government was gradually assuming more of the role of the family. Although the family survived as an important institution, the government extended more protection, initially to widows, children, and foreigners, but eventually to all members of the society. The increasing role of the government in the life of the individual marked a significant change from the earlier and more primitive Germanic customs.

Besides offering protection to the individual, the family remained the center around which the familial estate revolved. Laws of inheritance, therefore, preserved the integrity of the familial homestead, which passed from generation to generation. This custom was beginning to change in favor of the Church at the very time the Alamannic and Bavarian laws were promulgated. It became possible to give the homestead to a local church or monastery for the benefit of one's soul, but only after one's children had first received their legitimate share. A person who died in the service of his duke was guaranteed by law that his homestead would pass to his heirs uninhibited, and it was not permissable to enslave a freeman and disinherit his heirs. In fact, all children begotten by the same father, though having different mothers, were to receive an equal share of the paternal inheritance. The maternal inheritance, however, was divided according to the status of the mother, and children born to freemen by slave women were not to inherit equally with those children born by freewomen. A woman who married only once and was subsequently widowed was given a portion of her late husband's property equal to that given to her children. If there were no children, the widow received half her late husband's property; the other half reverted to the husband's relatives. Women who married a second time lost what property they retained from their former husbands, but were permitted to retain their morning gift (*morgangeba*), that is, a gift given to the wife the morning after the wedding night, which served as a pension in her old age.

The kindred, an entity larger than the immediate family in size, played an important role among the Alamans and Bavarians, as it did among all the Germanic peoples. Although there are no laws which specify how far the kindred extended, certainly it extended to at least the seventh generation, since inheritance of property was guaranteed up to the seventh degree of consanguinity. The kindred was especially prominent during land disputes. In these cases, a man could not press his claim unless other members of his kin were involved in the litigation. The involvement of the kindred in land disputes may have been the most cohesive way in which land was kept intact, as blood relatives assured that the homestead passed with little or no difficulty from generation to generation.

The value of women among the Alamans and Bavarians was, considered monetarily, twice that of the men, although this does not indicate that women were generally more favored in their society. The double estimate upon women applied only in cases in which men were subject to the same conditions; otherwise women had no favored status. This restriction is especially true for the compensation of crimes. Women were doubly compensated for those crimes of which men could also be the natural victim, such as murder or being sold into bondage. For those crimes to which men could not fall victim, and of which women would be the only victims, such as sexual abduction or a broken betrothal, women were compensated by the single standard sum. This was true for women from all three classes, slaves (maidservants), freedwomen, or freewomen. The schedule of legal compensation for women, therefore, does not indicate that they were more favored than men, since no victimized woman received double compensation for crimes that pertained exclusively to her sex. Indeed, the doubling of compensation reflected their relative powerlessness in society; women were defined as incapable of defending themselves with weapons.[5]

Supplemental to the twofold compensation of women, which, we may state firmly, indicated inferior status, was the institution of the *mundium.* Persons who did not have full legal rights— women, minors, orphans, foreigners, and slaves—were under the protection of able-bodied freemen, who exercised full legal rights in Alamannic and Bavarian societies. Unmarried daughters and children were under the protection of their fathers, brothers, and uncles; wives were under the protection of their husbands; slaves were under the protection of their masters; foreigners were under the protection of the government. Individuals under *mundium* lacked basic legal rights, including the right to defend oneself before one's peers in a court of law. Women and slaves, for example, could not accuse or be accused in court; they had no voice in the tribal assembly and had to speak through their legal guardians. In Germanic society, full legal rights belonged to those who could defend the weak through the force of arms.

There were two types of military recruitment among the Alamans and Bavarians, the general levy and the feudal vassal. The general levy required all able-bodied freemen to assemble with weapons and supplies at a specified time and place and to be ready when assembled to begin a military campaign, although it was nearly impossible to mobilize all the freemen at any one time. Few soldiers could be supplied with iron swords, helmets, and tunics, since only the wealthier classes could afford iron weapons. Most soldiers fought with simpler weapons, such as wooden spears or bows and arrows. Although originally the Germans fought on foot, armored cavalry was beginning to develop at the time the Alamannic and Bavarian laws were promulgated. The place where the army assembled was called the Marchfield (*Marciae Kalendae*) by the Alamannic laws, but it could meet at almost any time of the year. The Merovingian and Carolingian kings often led armies composed of subject peoples, such as the Alamans and Bavarians. The Alamannic laws specify that, on certain occasions, depending on the nature of the campaign, either the Frankish king or the Alamannic duke could lead the army. Soldiers who quarreled among themselves while serving in the army were faced with heavy fines under the Bavarian laws, particularly if people were slain because of such quarrels. Desertion was a treasonable offense and punishable by payment of the wergeld. Gradually, the army became feudalized, and there are illustrations of this development in the Alamannic and Bavarian laws. Cavalry, it can be seen, began to replace infantry, and specialized fighters were used instead of freemen at large. Insistence on discipline and morale replaced less stringent laws regulating people of diversified backgrounds, some of whom were reluctant to fight but were obligated to do so by law; it was against them that some of these laws were now directed. The new emphasis given to the war horse, specially bred for size and strength, should also be noted.

The laws of the Alamans and Bavarians that pertain to the duke are concerned that his sovereignty not be jeopardized. For this reason, most of these laws concern public law, and nearly all of the laws that directly concern the duke deal in one way or another with treason. Crimes such as conspiring to invade the duchy with foreign assistance, attempting to assassinate the duke, causing a rebellion within the army, deliberately disregarding ducal orders, or stealing property from the army or from the duke's courtyard, among others, are treasonable offenses in the

Alamannic and Bavarian laws. The duke served as the leading administrative, military, and judicial official in Alamannia and Bavaria, only to be supplanted eventually by the Merovingian and Carolingian kings. The duke could exploit the law to his own advantage, since it was legal to kill another while acting with ducal authority. The duke also led the army personally, and individual counts were directly responsible to him. He had the power to preside at the county court (*mallus*) or to appoint a representative to sit there on his behalf. In addition to the duties and responsibilities of the duke among the Alamans and Bavarians, the Bavarian laws set forth the genealogical preeminence of the duke and his immediate kin, and they are far more explicit in this regard than are the Alamannic laws. The Bavarian dukes were descendants of the aristocratic Agilolfinga family, which intermarried with the Merovingian Franks. Other related Bavarian aristocratic families, as enumerated by the Bavarian laws, were the Hosi, Draozza, Fagana, Hahilinga, and Anniona. Persons from these families received very high compensation for crimes committed against them, up to 640 solidi. If the Bavarian duke was killed, the law required that his relatives be paid 900 solidi as his wergeld. Assassination of the duke, therefore, meant almost certain death or debt slavery, since very few people or families could afford such a high wergeld.

Alamannia and Bavaria were divided into counties, each headed by a count, who in turn was directly responsible to the duke and who supplied the military forces needed by the duke for defense. Each count was accompanied by his own retinue (*comitatus*) of fighters, who owned allegiance directly to him. The count represented both civil and military powers; he not only led his troops on military campaigns, but presided in court as well. Counts were also responsible for maintaining the public peace, and therefore had police powers. A violation of the count's public authority was punishable by a fine of six solidi in the Alamannic laws. (The duke received twelve solidi for the same crime.) All of these functions made the count a very powerful public official who often exploited his power to his own advantage and who could even dispute his allegiance to the duke. By the mid-eighth century, when both the Alamannic and Bavarian laws were promulgated, the office of the count had become hereditary, as had that of the duke, but the loyalty of foreign dukes and counts was found wanting by the Franks, who replaced them with less autonomous officials.

Counties were also subdivided into hundreds (sing. *centena*), which were the judicial districts in which the hundred court took place. The hundred, therefore, became an administrative district, much like the county, although several hundreds were included in one county. The principal official of the hundred was the hundred-man (*centenarius*), who could call local freemen to arms if ordered by the count or duke, and who could command these troops himself for police action to apprehend a criminal. The hundred and the hundred-man may have become more powerful under Frankish influence. The public official under the hundred-man was the ten-man (*decanus*), whose primary function was to pursue and arrest criminals.

The guilt or innocence of anyone accused of committing a crime was determined before a county court (*mallus* or *placitum*), presided over by a judge (*iudex*), although the ultimate authority could be either the count or the *centenarius*. All freemen who resided within a particular county were obligated by law to attend the *mallus* when cases were brought before it. Since this obligation could be burdensome, freemen tried to avoid attending; however, freemen who refused to come to court were faced with heavy fines, twelve solidi in the Alamannic laws and fifteen in the Bavarian. Later, in 802, Charlemagne required freemen to attend only three meetings of the court each year.

The judicial procedure among the Alamans and Bavarians was commenced by the plantiff, who had the defendant summoned to court. It became the plantiff's responsibility to furnish proof to support his charge that the defendant was guilty. The plaintiff who failed to establish his charge was subject to the very penalty he accused the defendant of. The defendant proved his case not so much by the presentation of evidence, which in itself was important, but by taking an oath, which was supported by a predetermined number of oathtakers who believed in the defendant's innocence. The process of oathtaking was called compurgation. It was assumed that a man with a good reputation would have little difficulty in supplying the required number of oathtakers, which varied according to the gravity of the charge. A felony required more oathtakers than a less serious crime, and a defendant from a lower class needed more oathtakers than a defendant from a higher class. The oath carried far more importance than did the written word, for obvious reasons when we consider that the majority of Germans were illiterate. The defendant, therefore, cleared himself by swearing that he was innocent. The oath was taken upon some sacred object, usually at the altar of a church, or upon weapons, which were customarily consecrated. In the presentation of evidence, witnesses were also called forth to testify. They were expected to be reliable, tell the truth, and not be subject to bribes. Those witnesses who were known to have perjured themselves in the past were not allowed to testify in any future case before a court of law. Witnesses were needed in the confirmation of property to a church, in boundary disputes between two kindred, in proving that a child had been born alive but survived only a few hours after birth, in cases concerning attempts on the duke's life, in illegal construction of a building on another's property, in the confirmation of a sale of property, and in the validation of contracts between two parties. Individuals who testified falsely were subject to the punishment they would have inflicted on the accused.

If the court was dissatisfied with the oath, or if the accounts of the defendant and plaintiff conflicted strongly, the court put the defendant and plaintiff through an ordeal. Most conflicts of this nature were settled by the judicial duel, better known as the trial by combat (wager of battle). Both defendant and plaintiff appointed proven fighters to fight on their behalf in public in the presence of the judge. The fighters, usually with shield and sword, dueled, and the victor was declared innocent. That is, the party whose fighter won was assumed to have sworn his oath truthfully, since it was believed that truth would triumph over evil, and that God would not let the innocent be unjustly punished. The losing party of the duel stood accused of the crime presented originally before the court and paid the compensation. The object of the duel was to determine guilt or innocence, not to kill one's opponent.

The ordeal, which was used by all Germanic peoples, revealed the role of the supernatural in the judicial procedure. The ordeal of trial by combat (wager of battle) was used quite extensively by the Alamans and Bavarians, as it was by other Germanic nations, but other kinds of ordeal may also have been used, such as the ordeal of hot iron, in which a hot object was carried in the hand for a specified distance, or the ordeal of boiling water, in which a stone had to be pulled by the hand from the bottom of a vessel of boiling water. Guilt or innocence was determined by how rapidly the wound healed. Divine judgment was assumed to play an active role in the ordeal, in which the innocent party was expected to proceed confidently while the guilty did only with serious doubt. It should be noted, however, that a more skillful fighter or a person with more stamina and strength would be better suited to endure the ordeal. Although such procedures may seem illogical, the Germans (like many other primitive people) saw definite limits to what could and could not be known. Nevertheless, legal evidence was presented first, and the ordeal might or might not be used afterwards.

There may also have been some question as to the integrity of the judge, who, being human, could be subject to bribes. Although a judge derived an income from hearing cases, usually equal to one-ninth of the compensation required for a crime as indicated in the Bavarian laws, there are laws that indicate that dishonesty was far more profitable. Judges convicted of accepting bribes were required to pay double to the wronged party in the case, in addition to a fine payable to the duke. Judges who rendered judgments through ignorance were not guilty of a crime; but since they were expected to know the law, they were required to have a copy of the laws before them when they rendered justice. It was one of the principal concerns of the judges that oaths not be given too eagerly, and only after all evidence was presented. In most cases, the judge would be either the count or the *centenarius*.

An Alaman or Bavarian who could not obtain the required number of oathtakers could not defend himself in a court of law, and without this, he could not exercise his rights. It was, therefore, especially important that others valued and trusted his spoken word, since personal freedom was directly linked to its application. Oathtakers usually came from one's kin, and those who lacked sufficient numbers of oathtakers could not defend their case. If this happened, the defendant lost his case and could be declared outside the law's jurisdiction, that is, an outlaw.

The ideas of personal freedom within a class society, of compurgation, and of defense of individual freedom with force of arms are strongly related. All are extensions of the same principle—that a freeman exerted his rights to be free. If a freeman could not or did not exert his rights, he was not a freeman. Although rights might be initially conferred on a freeman, they had to be exercised in order to be retained. The two most obvious places where these rights were exercised were on the battlefield or in a private duel, and in court. The latter developed from the earlier institution of the tribal assembly, in which all freemen over the age of puberty proclaimed approval of a proposal by hitting their spears on their shields. Only freemen had this right, because only freemen could use weapons in their personal defense.

The Germanic legal codes concern social institutions, reflecting in large part social change and conflict; they offer less reflection of economic conditions. Fortunately for the study of the latter, other sources have survived, especially cartularies, copies of bequests given to monasteries and churches, which furnish much-needed information; these began to appear at the very time when the Germanic tribal laws ceased to be promulgated. In addition to cartularies, two exceptional legal codes survive which, unlike others, aid in the study of economic conditions—the Alamannic and Bavarian laws, respectively *L. Alam.* XXI and *L. Baiu.* I, 13. Both laws set down the manorial conditions under which indentured tenants, whether free *coloni* or slaves, worked for their lords. The agricultural conditions of both free and unfree laborers were approximately the same, that is, both were expected to render service and tribute. Service meant working three days a week for one's lord and three days for oneself. Tribute involved rendering certain quantities of food and supplies to one's lord, usually given in the form of chickens, eggs, bread, beer, linen, and the like. There are no manorial differences specified in either *L. Alam.* XXI or *L. Baiu.* I, 13 for *coloni* and slaves; both appear to do the same kind of service, and both render the same amount of tribute. This is especially important since the distinction between free and unfree manorial tenants did not begin to disappear in other parts of western Europe until a half century later, in the mid-ninth century, when the tenants formed one class defined by function. Alamannia and Bavaria spearheaded this development by the mid-eighth century.[6] The agricultural conditions set down in the Alamannic and Bavarian laws indicated a rural, not an urban, society.

During the time the Alamannic and Bavarian laws were promulgated, ecclesiastical and secular landowners were acquiring more land at the expense of the poorer class of freemen. This happened because of pressure brought to bear by wealthy landowners, crop failure and impending famine, or debt. All of these caused the decline of the *alod* (*allod*), land which was owned outright by a freeman and from which no obligations were owed to another. It was this land that was relinquished to an ecclesiastical or secular lord in exchange for economic security in an uncertain age. The freemen who relinquished their land to wealthy landowners received the land back as a *precarium,* became indentured tenants, and performed mandatory obligations of tribute and service. Military service was also required from free tenants who worked for a landowner, since the latter was obliged to supply troops for military campaigns. This obligation developed rapidly throughout the late eighth century, and it was at this time that military obligations linked with economic dependency led to the beginning of feudalism. There are traces of the early medieval origins of feudalism in both the Alamannic and Bavarian laws.

Domestic animals were a chief source of wealth for the Alamans and Bavarians, in addition to land. There are innumerable references to domestic animals in the laws. The most common livestock were oxen, horses, sheep, pigs, and goats. Oxen were used principally for plowing and drawing wagons, but horses were used as draft animals (*iumentum*), particularly for transportation of people and light baggage. Horses were bred for many purposes. The larger and stronger horses were used for war, whereas the smaller and weaker horses were used as draft animals. The compensation for animals, like other kinds of property, depended on their value. In the Alamannic laws a war horse, for example, was appraised up to four times the value of an ordinary draft horse. Cows were used primarily for milk, but if they suffered mortal injury, they would be eaten. Pigs and sheep, not cattle, were the principal sources of meat, but this pertained almost exclusively to the wealthier classes, since the poorer classes ate mostly grain. Chickens were another common domestic animal. Moreover, the Alamans and Bavarians expended considerable care on the domestication of dogs and birds. For example, there were several different breeds of hunting dogs, in addition to greyhounds, bloodhounds, dachshunds, sheep dogs, and the common household watchdog. Of birds, the most important was the hawk, which was used to attack and capture several other birds, especially ducks, geese, and cranes. Jays, storks, ravens, crows, doves, and cuckoos were also described, and there were even songbirds that the wealthy domesticated. There were also certain wild animals that were of value, particularly deer and boars. Although the laws do not specify what purpose these animals served, it may be assumed that they were used as food.

Another institution of the Alamans and Bavarians, like other

Germans, was the offering of pledged property as security for debt payments. There were, therefore, two parties involved in every pledge, the pledger, or debtor, and the pledgee, or creditor. The pledge given to the pledgee equalled the value of the property that would actually satisfy the debt. In case the pledger could not pay the debt, the pledge would become a valid substitution. Pledges could be of two kinds, pledges of chattels and pledges of land; the former was the older of the two. To be valid, pledging had to occur in the presence of the judge. Most types of property pledged were pigs, sheep, horses, cattle, and slaves. There may also have been other pledged property although the laws do not specify them. The pledgee (creditor) could not destroy, use, or sell the pledge. Pledges were a form of security that gave the creditor possession, although not ownership, of the pledged property. Pledges were also offered by witnesses as security in court to confirm that they would testify truthfully. It was illegal to forcibly detain a person as a pledge. If the pledger legally pledged property and the pledge (say, a slave or an animal) caused damage or death, the pledger was required to make restitution. However, if the pledgee illegally received a pledge, he was held responsible for any damage the pledge may have caused. In the latter case, the pledger was not held responsible.

There is no evidence that the Alamans and Bavarians minted coins. They used Merovingian, and, later, Carolingian coins, as well as coins struck by the Lombard kings. The coins they used were the three principal coins of the early Middle Ages: the *solidus, tremissis,* and *saiga.* All of these were made of gold; one solidus equalled three tremisses or twelve saigae. There was also a fourth coin, the *denarius* (silver penny), but the Alamannic and Bavarian laws each refer to the denarius only once. Four denarii equalled one tremissis. All these coins were of small denomination; there were none higher. Although these coins were used to compensate for crimes, other forms of wealth, such as livestock, could also be used. The average person would rarely have a few solidi in his possession, since even a large quantity of this small coin was beyond his means. The excessive fines required for crimes had to be paid not only from one's own estate, but also from the estates of one's kin.

The Christian Church exerted a considerable influence on the Alamannic and Bavarian laws. Not only did the clergy aid in promulgating these legal codes, but they also added laws that protected themselves and church property from injury. These laws supply us with little information outside their immediate subject matter. The ecclesiastical laws, *L. Alam.* I–XXII and *L. Baiu.* I, 1–13, 14 [VII, 3a], introduce both law codes and contain similar concepts. The Bavarian laws contain several biblical references, but the Alamannic laws contain none, and the Bavarian laws indicate stronger ecclesiastical influence. The Church in Alamannia and Bavaria was concerned principally with maintaining the legitimacy of property bestowed to a church, protecting the right of sanctuary to fugitives (usually slaves), protecting church property from arson or theft, and protecting the clergy from physical harm. The Church applied both secular and ecclesiastical punishment to those who jeopardized the clergy or its property. Not only were violators made to pay the wergeld and monetary compensation, but they were also threatened with excommunication.

EDITIONS AND MANUSCRIPTS

Alamannic laws and *Pactus legis Alamannorum*

The Alamannic laws are available in the edition of Karl Lehmann (1888) and two editions by Karl August Eckhardt (1934 and 1962). Eckhardt has also revised the edition of Lehmann for the *Monumenta Germaniae Historica* (1966). Eckhardt (1934) renders a modern German translation with his Latin edition of the Alamannic laws. The English translation furnished in this book is based on the most comprehensive edition of the Alamannic laws, that of the revised edition of Karl Lehmann (1966). (See the list of abbreviations above for the editions of the Alamannic laws.)

The manuscripts of the Alamannic laws are classified into three different traditions: the *Lex Alamannorum Lantfridana, Lex Alamannorum Hlotharii,* and *Lex Alamannorum Karolina.* The English translation included in this book is based on the first of the traditions, although both the Hlotharii and Karolina have been consulted in rendering it, particularly on Codex 8 of the Lantfridana manuscripts. (The Lantfridana manuscripts are named after the Alamannic Duke Lantfrid [712–30] under whose personal direction the last redaction of the Alamannic laws was undertaken; the Hlotharii manuscripts are named after the Merovingian King Chlotar IV [717–19], during whose reign the Alamannic laws were promulgated; the Karolina manuscripts are named after Charlemagne [768–814], who may have revised the Alamannic laws about 788.[7]) This English translation also contains the *Pactus legis Alamannorum,* which was, so to speak, the first edition (ca. 613) of the Alamannic laws. Since several laws of the *Lex Alamannorum* are taken verbatim from the *Pactus,* references to the latter are indicated in the margins of corresponding Alamannic laws.

Much as the Bavarian laws, the Alamannic laws supply an introductory list briefly describing the laws (or titles, as they are properly called), which summarizes the contents of individual laws; the exceptions are laws VII and XXXIII, which are not furnished with descriptions. The list of titles appears before the prologue and the text. In the English translation that follows, not only has the introductory list of title descriptions been included, but the descriptions have been added before each law in the *Lex Alamannorum.* The titular descriptions, which do not form part of the original text, are presented within brackets. The laws contain their own internal divisions (save for the first, which concerns ecclesiastical law, titles I–XXII); title XXIII is prefaced with the description, "Concerning cases that pertain to the duke," which heads ducal law (titles XXIII–XLIII); and title XLIV is prefaced with the description, "Concerning disputes that commonly occur among the people," which heads private law (titles XLIV–XCVIII).

There are a few lacunae in both the Lantfridana and Hlotharii manuscripts of the Alamannic laws. Although a three-part division of law V is furnished in this translation, it is derived not from the Lantfridana, but from the Karolina manuscripts. The Lantfridana manuscripts render only a very short law, and only in part, of the larger three-part division of law V. Both the Lantfridana and Hlotharii manuscripts lack a law found only in the Karolina manuscripts, which is renumbered Va in this translation. (The Karolina manuscripts number this law VI, but it has to be renumbered to be placed between laws V and VI. Eckhardt's edition also renumbers it V a.)

Bavarian laws

There are three modern editions of the Bavarian laws—the editions of Konrad Beyerle (1926), Ernst von Schwind (1926), and Karl August Eckhardt (1934).[8] Beyerle's and Eckhardt's editions are accompanied by modern German translations, but there is no comparable translation into any other modern language. The English translation furnished in this book is based on the most critical edition of the text, that of Konrad Beyerle (1926). (See the list of abbreviations above for the editions of the Bavarian laws.) Beyerle's edition contains a photographic reproduction of the oldest surviving manuscript of the laws, known as the Ingolstadt Manuscript, with an accompanying German translation. The Ingolstadt Manuscript (Codex Ms. 132) is now in the library of the University of Munich. The manuscript was willed by Dr. Christoph Gewold (1556–1621) to the university library at Ingolstadt on his death in 1621. It was acquired by the University of Munich in 1825.

The Ingolstadt Manuscript is thought to have been written about the beginning of the ninth century, which places it approximately fifty years after the promulgation of the laws of Duke Odilo, the reigning Bavarian duke in whose lifetime the final redaction of the laws appeared. The traditional date given for the promulgation of the laws is 744–48. The laws are referred to as a complete text in the reign of the Bavarian Duke Tassilo III (748–88). Since they show strong Frankish influence, they must have been promulgated after the Bavarians had lost their independence, which occurred in 744. Hence, the laws are thought to have appeared between 744 and 748, and the reigning Bavarian duke at that time was Odilo (739–48).

The Ingolstadt Manuscript divides the Bavarian laws into twenty-three divisions or major titles. Other manuscripts contain one major title less, or twenty-two titles. Each of these is subdivided into several individual laws. In all, the Bavarian laws contain 273 laws, most concerning criminal law, divided into three topical divisions. Title I concerns ecclesiastical law, especially in regard to church property in Bavaria; titles II and III concern public law, especially in regard to the Bavarian duke and the government; and titles IV–XXIII (IV–XXII in manuscripts other than the Ingolstadt) concern private law, particularly criminal and family law. The principal offenses detailed in the laws are treason, murder, abduction, theft, arson, and sexual assault.

Unfortunately, several pages of the Ingolstadt Manuscript are missing. Beyerle supplied the missing parts of the Ingolstadt manuscript from other manuscripts, although he supplied a full German translation. The missing passages are: part of laws II, 4, 5, IX, 2, 4, XV, 3, 8, 10, and XVI, 3, and all of laws IX, 3, XV,

4–7, and XVI, 1, 2. Later manuscripts make occasional additions to or modifications of the text, either clarifying its vocabulary or rearranging its sentences into better logical order. The later additions and modifications have been incorporated into this English translation if they make more sense than the text originally contained in the Ingolstadt Manuscript. These modifications can be seen in the editions of Schwind and Eckhardt.

Like the Alamannic laws, the Ingolstadt Manuscript of the Bavarian laws supplies an introductory list of title descriptions, and these are appended within brackets before individual laws in this translation. There are no title descriptions for laws V, VI, and XX–XXIII, and therefore no corresponding descriptions are interpolated before these laws. The only law deliberately put in a new position in the text is I, 14, which is often renumbered VII, 3a. Although I, 14, which prohibits servile work on Sundays, logically is included in the first title, which concerns ecclesiastical law, it is usually placed in title VII, which is primarily concerned with the prohibition of illicit marriages and related matters concerning the Church. Law I, 14 is renumbered VII, 3a in this translation to bring it into agreement with later manuscripts.

Because there are overwhelming similarities between the Alamannic and Bavarian laws, legal references to the former have been included in the margins of corresponding Bavarian laws. Of the 273 laws in Beyerle's edition of the Ingolstadt Manuscript, 100 laws show striking similarity to the Alamannic laws. Lehmann's editions of the Alamannic laws (1888/1962) give 275 laws. The similarity in the number of laws between the Alamannic and Bavarian laws is remarkable, since no other Germanic legal code contains nearly as many.

CONCLUSION

In translating the Alamannic and Bavarian laws, a number of difficulties had to be overcome. Apart from the obvious difficulty of producing a modern English translation of two Latin legal codes, both twelve centuries old, there are several special legal concepts and Germanic terms that present particular problems. Although a few specialized terms have been left in Latin, most Latin terms have been rendered English equivalents. Germanic terms are retained in the original language, but the Glossary at the end of the book supplies English translations with bibliographical references. The translation provided in this book stays as close as possible to the original Latin without producing awkward English.

A study of the early Middle Ages is greatly aided by a study of Germanic law, since it is principally through the *leges barbarorum* that Germanic custom has come down to us. Apart from cartularies and occasional references in contemporary histories and annals, the early Middle Ages offer little additional information about Germanic custom. The survival of the *leges barbarorum* allows us an insight into primitive Germanic society that would not be possible otherwise.

NOTES

[1] In general, see Simeon L. Guterman, *From Personal to Territorial Law: Aspects of the History and Structure of the Western Legal-Constitutional Tradition* (Metuchen, 1972).

[2] See Ernst Levy, *West Roman Vulgar Law: The Law of Property, Memoirs of the American Philosophical Society,* 29 (Philadelphia, 1951), and his *Weströmisches Vulgarrecht das Obligationenrecht, Forschungen zum römischen Recht,* 7 (Weimar, 1956).

[3] For the historical background of the Alamannic and Bavarian laws, see Heinrich Brunner, *Deutsche Rechtsgeschichte,* 2d ed., 2 vols. (Leipzig, 1906–28), 1: 448–54 and 454–64 respectively. Also see Rudolf Buchner, *Die Rechtsquellen,* Beiheft to Wilhelm Wattenbach and Wilhelm Levison, *Deutschlands Geschichtsquellen im Mittelalter, Vorzeit und Karolinger* (Weimar, 1953), pp. 29–33 and 26–29 respectively.

[4] The importance of these similarities is discussed in detail in my unpublished doctoral dissertation, "Contributions to the Criticism and Interpretation of the 'Lex Baiuvariorum': A Comparative Study of the Alamannic and Bavarian Codes" (Fordham University 1973). It should be noted in passing that the English translation furnished in this book is based on Beyerle's edition of the Ingolstadt Ms., but my doctoral dissertation is based on the edition of Schwind. Consequently, my treatment of the Alamannic-Bavarian similarities here differs on a few points from that given in my dissertation.

[5] See my "Legal Status of Freewomen in the Lex Alamannorum," *Zeitschrift der Savigny-Stiftung für Rechtsgeschichte, Germanistische Abteilung* 91 (1974): 175–79. Although this article concerns the Alamannic laws, it makes several comparisons to the Bavarian laws in its footnotes.

[6] See my "Seigneurial Obligations and 'Lex Baiuvariorum' I, 13," *Traditio* 31 (1975): 336–43.

[7] See Karl von Amira, *Germanisches Recht,* 4th rev. ed., Karl August Eckhardt, Grundriss der germanischen Philologie, 5, 1 (Berlin, 1960), 1: 59.

[8] Rudolf Buchner is re-editing the Bavarian laws for the *Monumenta Germaniae Historica;* his will replace the edition of Schwind. Reference is given in the *Deutsches Archiv für Erforschung des Mittelalters* 30 (1974): iv.

Pactus Legis Alamannorum

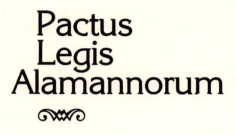

The Compact of the Alamannic Laws.

Here begins the compact of the Alamannic laws, and thus it is resolved [in the year of our . . .] lord king Chlotar[1], where there were thirty-three dukes and thirty-three bishops and forty-five counts.

I.

1. If anyone breaks another's head so that the brain appears, let him pay twelve solidi.[2]

2. And if a claim that the blow was not a major one arises between them over this altercation, yet a physician still inquires about this injury, let the physician take a solemn oath with his iron tools or find three witnesses who affirm this.

3. But if neither the witnesses affirm nor the physician swears, let him [the accused] pay six solidi or swear with six men, half of whom are chosen, that he owes him [the other] no more compensation.

4. If anyone breaks another's head so that a bone of the head is separated and [when thrown] it sounds against a shield held by someone on the road, let him pay six solidi or swear with six men, half of whom are chosen.

5. If it is such a blow that he scratches his head and breaks a

bone there, let him pay three solidi or swear with three men, half of whom are chosen.

II.

1. If a freeman [strikes a freeman . . .]³
7. If anyone strikes a freewoman with a blow and blood does not flow, let him pay two solidi.
8. If she is a freedwoman, one solidus and a tremissis.⁴
9. If she is a maidservant, let him pay one solidus.
10. If he is a man [*baro*], similarly.
11. If he is a slave, one-half solidus.

III.⁵

IV.⁶

V.

1. And if anyone injures another's eye and the eye remains in place, let him pay twenty solidi.
2. If the eye comes forward, [let him pay] forty solidi or let him swear with twelve men, half of whom are chosen.

VI.

1. And he who mutilates an ear, let him pay twenty solidi.
2. If he cuts off the entire [ear] or if he injures it so that [the victim] cannot hear, let him pay forty solidi or swear with twelve men.

VII.

1. If anyone pierces an arm above the elbow, let him pay six solidi.
2. If it is below the elbow, let him pay three solidi.
3. In a similar manner, if a hip is pierced, let him pay six solidi.
4. If [a leg is pierced] below the knee, let him pay three solidi.
5. If it is not pierced, but he still strikes the muscle so that body fluid enters [the wound] there, let him pay three solidi.
6. If [he pierces] an arm above the elbow or a leg⁷ above the knee, similar compensation.

VIII.

1. [If] anyone is injured internally in his chest or his side, let the perpetrator pay twelve solidi or swear with twelve men, half of whom are chosen.

2. If he is pierced, let the perpetrator pay twenty-four solidi or swear with twelve men.

3. If anyone pierces another in his side in such a manner that [the victim] does not suffer internal injury, let him pay six solidi or swear with six men, half of whom are chosen.

IX.

1. If anyone breaks but does not cripple another's arm above the elbow or leg[8] above the knee with a sword or stick, let him pay six solidi.

2. And if he [breaks] but does not cripple [an arm] below the elbow or [a leg] below the knee, let him pay three solidi.

3. If he strikes the muscle and body fluid enters [the wound], let him pay three solidi.

4. If anyone cripples another's arm, let him pay twenty solidi.

5. And if he cuts it off, let him pay forty solidi or swear with twelve men.

X.

1. If anyone cuts off another's thumb, let him pay twelve solidi.

2. If he cripples or cuts off [the thumb] at the first joint, let him pay six solidi.

3. If the second finger is cut off, let him pay ten solidi.

4. If he cripples it, let him pay five solidi.

5. If it is cut off at the first joint, let him pay three solidi.

6. If the third finger is cut off, let him pay six solidi.

7. If he cripples it, let him pay three solidi.

8. If the fourth finger is cut off, let him pay five solidi.

9. If it is cut off at the first joint, let him pay three solidi.

10. If the little finger is cut off, let him pay ten solidi.

11. If he cripples it, let him pay five solidi.

12. And if the hand is pierced, let him pay six solidi.

13. And if an entire hand is cut off, let him pay forty solidi or swear with twelve men, half of whom are chosen.

XI.

1. If anyone cuts off another's foot, let him pay forty solidi.
2. And if he cripples it, let him pay twenty solidi.
3. And if he can walk outside his estate and can walk in his field with a crutch [*stelzia*], let the perpetrator pay twenty-five solidi or swear with twelve men, half of whom are chosen.
4. If anyone cuts off another's big toe, let him pay six solidi.
5. If it is cut off at the first joint, let him pay three solidi.
6. If it happens to a freedman, let him pay four solidi.
7. If to a slave, let him pay three solidi.
8. If other toes are cut off, let him pay three solidi [for each].

XII.

If any woman is pregnant and through the act of another the child is born dead, or if it is born alive but does not live for nine nights, let him who is accused pay forty solidi or swear with twelve men, half of whom are chosen.

XIII.

1. If a woman calls another a witch or a poisoner, whether it is said in a dispute [in the presence of the accused] or in one's absence, let her pay twelve solidi.
2. If a woman calls a man deceitful without due cause, let her pay twelve solidi or let her husband swear with twelve men, half of whom are chosen.

XIV.

1. If anyone accuses a freewoman of the crime of witchcraft or poisoning and seizes her and puts her in a hurdle, let him compensate eighty solidi, and let her be defended by her relatives with twelve men, half of whom are chosen, or with a drawn sword.
2. If it is a maidservant, let her be compensated fifteen solidi.
3. If she [a freewoman] is not put in a hurdle, [but] is seized and tortured, let him compensate with forty solidi.
4. And if she [a maidservant] is not put in a hurdle, let him pay six solidi.
5. And if a man finds her guilty and because of this she is killed, let him pay the same [her] wergeld,[9] since he accused the woman.

6. If it is a man [*baro*] from the lower class [*minoflidis*], let him pay 160 solidi.

7. If it is an Alaman from the middle class, let him compensate with 200 solidi.

8. If it is an Alaman from the upper class, let him compensate with 240 solidi or swear with twenty-four men, half of whom are chosen, or with forty, whomever he can find.

9. If the woman was from the lower class [*minoflidus*], let him pay 320 solidi.

10. If she is from the middle class, let him pay 400 solidi.

11. If she is an Alaman from the upper class, let him pay 480 solidi.

XV.

If anyone murders [*mortaudus fuerit*][10] a man [*baro*] or a woman who is [free], let a lawful wergeld be paid ninefold, or let the doer swear with twenty-four men, all chosen, or with eighty, whomever he can find.

XVI.

1. If anyone removes property worth a solidus from a corpse in a grave, let him pay forty solidi.

2. And if it is worth one or two tremisses, let him pay twelve solidi or swear with twelve men, half of whom are chosen.

3. And [if] something is removed or stolen from a grave where a person rests, whether the dead man was killed or died naturally, let him [the thief] restore what he stole there and pay eighty solidi if he exhumed the corpse and plundered the grave.

XVII.

1. If any freeman kills a freeman and steals anything of his property from him [and][11] offers this to his own relatives, it is not to be acquired.

2. But if he does not offer [this property], let him pay forty solidi.

3. If [the victim is] a freedman, manumitted in a church or by relatives in the army, let the perpetrator compensate with thirteen solidi and a tremissis.

4. If it is done to a slave, let the perpetrator compensate with twelve solidi.

5. If it is done to a free Alamannic woman, let him compensate with eighty solidi or swear with twelve men.

6. If it is a freedwoman, let him compensate with twenty-six solidi and two tremisses.

7. If it is a maidservant, let him compensate with twelve solidi or swear with twelve men, half of whom are chosen.

XVIII.

1. Concerning waylayers [*wegalaugen*], [if a man blocks the way of a freeman], let him pay six solidi.

2. If it is a freedman [who is blocked], let the perpetrator pay four solidi.

3. If it is a slave, three solidi.

4. If he does this to a free Alamannic woman, let him compensate with twelve solidi.

5. If it is a freedwoman, let him compensate with eight solidi.

6. If it is a maidservant, let him pay four solidi.

7. If a man seizes her hair, [let him compensate similarly].

XIX.

1. If anyone intrudes upon another's property or a church in an illegal manner, the man who repels the violence being done commits no crime, since one does no violence defending his own property.

2. Let no one attempt [to intrude upon] another's land without authority; let him who does this know that he is to be expelled with punishment.

XX.

1. If anyone steals a mill iron, let him replace it along with another and pay six solidi for this theft to him whose it was.

2. If anyone breaks or steals another's wheel hub, let him pay three solidi.

3. If he steals a cart or breaks the front wheels so that on that day work is hindered, let him compensate with three solidi.

4. If he steals or breaks the rear [wheels], let him compensate with six solidi.

5. If it is a harrow, let him compensate with three solidi.

XXI.

1. If anyone burns a shelter in a forest, whether it is for pigs or cattle, let him compensate with twelve[12] solidi.

2. And if he enters with the intention of doing harm and finds nothing of the owner's, let him compensate with six solidi.

3. And if he enters another's courtyard, [let him compensate] in a similar manner.

4. If [he enters] a storehouse, let him compensate with twelve solidi.

5. If a murderer flees into a courtyard or house, and no one offers a surety for him, and if his pursuer follows him there, he is not to make a claim [against the murderer].

XXII.

1. If anyone offers a herd of pigs, draft horses, cows, or sheep as a pledge, let him be liable for forty solidi.

2. If a bound swineherd is struck or beaten on the road, and two hold him and a third strikes him, let the swineherd be compensated with nine solidi.

3. And for the rest that he suffers, let him be compensated threefold as [is compensated] for slaves.

4. For herdsmen of sheep, horses, and cows, let them be compensated twofold as [is compensated] for slaves.

XXIII.

1. If anyone steals or kills a bison, a buffalo, [or] a stag that bellows, let him compensate with twelve solidi.

2. And [if] that stag does not have shackles, let him [the perpetrator] compensate with one-half solidus.

3. If it has a shackle and is not [killed] by arrows, let him pay one solidus.

4. If a red deer [is killed] by arrows, let him pay three solidi.

5. If a black [deer], let him compensate with six solidi.

6. If it is stolen, let him compensate ninefold.

XXIV.

1. If a wild doe is killed, let him [the perpetrator] pay a tremissis.

2. If it has a shackle, one-half solidus.

3. If a red doe [is killed] by arrows, let him pay three solidi.

4. If a black [doe], let him pay six solidi.

5. If it is stolen, let him compensate ninefold.

XXV.

1. If another's bear is killed or stolen, let him pay six solidi.

2. For a wild boar, similarly.

3. If anyone kills a domesticated cow, which is called a lead cow, a boar, or a lead hog, let him compensate with six solidi.

4. If it is stolen, let him pay three solidi; and whatever he [the owner] swears it is worth, let him compensate eightfold [that is, if it is not returned].

5. If anyone kills a roebuck, a saiga.[13]

6. If it is stolen, let him compensate ninefold.

XXVI.

1. If a crane is stolen or killed, let him compensate with three solidi.

2. If a goose is stolen or killed, let him pay ninefold.

3. For a duck, jay, stork, raven, crow, dove, and cuckoo, let [compensation] be required as for other similar [birds].

4. If a hawk kills a goose, let its owner pay three solidi.

5. If [it kills] a crane, let its owner compensate with six solidi.

XXVII.

If a boar kills another boar, let another be returned for it or let three solidi be paid.

XXVIII.

1. If another's dog kills a man, let its owner pay half the wergeld.

2. And if the relatives of the deceased seek the entire wergeld, let all his [the owner of the dog] doors be closed, and let him always enter and leave through one door; and let the dog be hung nine feet above that entrance until it becomes completely putrefied, and drops decayed matter, and its bones lie there. And he cannot enter or leave through any other door. And if he re-

moves the dog from the entrance or enters the house through another door, let him return the other half of the wergeld.

XXIX.

1. If a horse, pig, or ox kills a man, let its owner pay the entire wergeld.

2. If it is a slave [who is killed], let him pay half the slave's price.

XXX.

1. If someone's horse jumps over another's fence and is pierced by a stake, let him who owns the fence pay half the price.

2. If anyone hacks another's fence, let him pay three solidi.

XXXI.

1. If anyone buries a corpse in foreign ground, let him pay twelve solidi or swear with twelve men that he did not do this with malice.

2. If anyone sends a freeman or freewoman into another's land without permission from him to whom the land belongs, let him be liable for forty solidi.

3. If he is a slave, let him pay twelve solidi.

4. If anyone [injures] the child of a person from the lower class, let him pay a solidus.

5. If [the child] is from the middle class, let him pay six solidi.

6. If from the highest class, let him pay twelve solidi.

XXXII.

1. If anyone violently abducts another's girl, let him be liable for her wergeld.

2. If she is not raped [but is still abducted], let him pay forty solidi.

XXXIII.[14]

XXXIV.

1. If any woman is killed, leaving no descendants by her husband, let all her property, whatever was legally obtained, be returned to the relatives.

2. And if she survives her husband, let all the bedding be removed by her.

3. If she wishes to depart freely, let her take what she legally obtained. Let the bedding be equally divided.

XXXV.

1. If a husband dismisses his wife, let him compensate her with forty solidi, and have no [more] authority over her guardianship [*mundium*], and return all things to her that she legally obtained.

2. If he keeps anything, let this woman have authority over the property and let him pay twelve solidi.

3. Concerning any thing as small as a fibula [*nastula, brooch*], which is legally hers, let the husband swear or return it.

XXXVI.

1. If anyone angrily seizes another's hand or clothing, let him pay six solidi.

2. If anyone throws another from a horse, let him pay six solidi.

XXXVII.

1. If he kills another's pledge [a cow],[15] let him pay six solidi.

2. If it is a pig or sheep, let him pay three solidi.

XXXVIII.

1. If a man gives one pledge in place of another or steals a pledge out of anger, let him compensate with a tremissis, that is, if he took a cow from a yoked herd.

2. If it is unyoked, let two saigae be compensated.

3. If it is a horse, one solidus.

4. If it is a greyhound, one-half solidus.

5. If it is a draft horse, a tremissis.

6. If it is removed, let him compensate similarly.

XXXIX.

1. If anyone binds another and sells him outside the borders [*marcha*], let him restore him to that place and compensate with forty solidi.

2. If he cannot find him, let him pay his wergeld.

XL.

1. If anyone takes a stallion from a herd and castrates it, let him pay as many solidi as the horse is worth.

2. If anyone removes another's draft horse from a herd and harnesses it, let him restore one of equal value to the owner.

3. If it is killed, let him pay three solidi.

4. If it is an average mare, let him compensate with six solidi.

5. If it is of the highest value, let him compensate with twelve solidi.

6. If it is a bull, let him compensate with six solidi.

7. If it is stolen, let him compensate with six solidi and also compensate as much as eightfold its value.

XLI.

1. If a blacksmith is killed, let the perpetrator compensate with forty solidi.

2. If it is a goldsmith, let the perpetrator compensate with fifty solidi.

3. If any of them is crippled, let the perpetrator compensate with fifteen solidi.

XLII.

1. If anyone begins to harvest another's crops, let him compensate with twelve solidi or swear with twelve men that he did not do this because of spite.

2. [If] he takes crops through enmity, let him pay three solidi.

NOTES

[1] Chlotar II was king of Neustria (northwestern kingdom) from 584–629 and sole king of all Merovingian Gaul from 613 to his death in 629. In 613, Chlotar II held a court at Marlenheim and may have promulgated an edition of the *Pactus legis Alamannorum* at this time. The reference to the court at Marlenheim is found in *The Fourth Book of the Chronicle of Fredegar and its Continuations,* ed. and trans. J. M. Wallace-Hadrill, Nelson Medieval Texts (London, 1960), p. 36 (Fredegar, *Chronicle,* 4, 43).

[2] A *solidus* (pl. *solidi*) is a gold coin, equal to three *tremisses* or twelve *saigae.* For this and other Latin terms, see the Glossary.

[3] Part of law II, 1 and all of II, 2–6 are missing from the Pactus.

[4] A *tremissis* (pl. *tremisses*) is a gold coin, worth four times the value of the *saiga*.

[5] The laws are missing from the manuscript. Cf. Lex LVII, 57–59.

[6] The laws are missing from the manuscript. Cf. Lex LVII, 15–30.

[7] Although hip (*coxa*) is given in the law, it does not fit the context. It is necessarily a leg, not a hip, that is pierced above the knee.

[8] See n. 7 above.

[9] *Wergeld* is the price of a person's life, which varied with his class (slave, freed, free) and was usually computed in the form of money. This system of monetary payment was intended to prevent blood feuds between individuals or families.

[10] See the Glossary for this and other Germanic terms.

[11] The text gives *aut* (or), but should be read *et* (and); Lehmann supplies *et* in his collation.

[12] Alternate mss. give twenty-two solidi. Lex XCIV, 1, which is derived verbatim from Pactus XXI, 1, also gives twenty-two solidi.

[13] A *saiga* (pl. *saigae*) is a small gold coin, twelve of which equal one *solidus*.

[14] The laws are missing.

[15] The law does not specify what kind of animal is pledged, but it would probably be cattle. Pigs and sheep are discussed in Pactus XXXVII, 2.

The
Alamannic Laws
as derived from the
Lantfridana
Manuscripts

Here begin the chapters of the Alamannic laws.

LXXII–LXXIII [LXXIX]. If anyone kills a swineherd.

LXXV [LXXX]. If anyone violates another's chambermaid.

LXXVI–LXXVII [LXXXI]. If anyone sets another's house on fire at night.

LXXVIII [LXXXII]. Concerning the stealing of hunting dogs.

LXXIX [LXXXIII]. Concerning the building of a dam in water.

LXXX [LXXXIV]. Concerning a mill [or any] dam in water.

LXXXI [LXXXV]. If a dispute arises between kindred.

LXXXII [LXXXVI]. If anyone receives a fugitive and does not wish to restore him to his master.

LXXXIII [LXXXVII]. Concerning injurious pledges.

LXXXIV [LXXXVIII]. If anyone [refuses to return] another's property.

LXXXV [LXXXIX]. Do not let one brother dissipate another brother's property before they divide [the paternal inheritance].

LXXXVI [XC]. Concerning swearing for homicide.

LXXXVII [XCI]. Concerning the cutting off [of the lef] at the knee.

LXXXVIII [XCII]. Concerning an abortion in a woman.

LXXXIX [XCIII]. If a woman dies after childbirth, leaving an heir.

XC [XCIV]. If anyone leaves his peer fighting and flees.

XCI [XCV]. If anyone wishes to summon [another] after a case is settled.

XCII [XCVI]. If anyone strikes a freewoman with a blow.

XCIII [XCVII]. Concerning the stealing of a wheel hub or cart.

XCIV, 1–3 [XCVIII]. If anyone burns or enters a shelter.

XCIV, 4 [XCIX]. If anyone offers a herd of pigs or draft horses or cows as a pledge.

In the name of Christ here begins the text of the
Alamannic laws, which were renewed in the time of
Lantfrid,[1] son of Godofrid.
Here begins this text.[2]

I.

[If (anyone hands over) his property or himself to a church.]

1. If any freeman wishes to hand over his property or himself to a church, let no one, neither the duke, nor the count, nor any person, have permission to prohibit him, but let it be permitted for a Christian man to serve God of his own free will and to redeem himself with his own property. And whoever wishes to do this, let him confirm it through a charter in which he expresses his wish to give his property to a church, and let him call six or seven witnesses; and let the charter contain their names, and let him place it on the altar in the presence of the priest who serves that church; and let the ownership of that property always remain with that church.[3]

2. And if any person, either he who gives it or any of his heirs, wishes afterwards to remove that property from the church, or if any man or any person attempts to do this, let him suffer the judgment of God and excommunication of the Holy Church; and let him not attain the goal that he seeks; and let him pay the fine that the charter contains; and let him return the property intact; and let him pay the *fredus*[4] to the state as the law requires.

II.

[If any of his property, which he gives to a church, (is returned) as a benefice to him by a bishop.]

1. If any freeman who gives his property to a church and confirms it through a charter, as is stated above, afterwards receives it as a benefice from the priest of the church in order to provide

the necessary subsistence all the days of his life, let him pay to the church the tribute of the land he pledged, and let this be done through a letter of confirmation, so that after his death none of his relatives may contest this act. And if it happens that after his death there is, by chance, a surviving son who wishes to say that his father's inheritance legitimately belongs to his possession and his father neither gave nor confirmed it, let him not be allowed to swear, but let the charter that his father made be presented, and let those witnesses who placed their hands on the charter together with the priest of the church, as the law requires, testify that they were present and saw with their eyes and heard with their ears that his father gave that property to the church and made a charter and called them as witnesses. Let them say this by an oath: "We are true witnesses." After this, let the priest of the church take possession of this property, and let the objector pay to the church the fine that the charter contains.

2. If, however, the charter that was originally made is burned or lost, then let it be permitted for that heir with five designated witnesses and himself as a sixth to swear in the church that his father neither made a charter nor gave it to that holy place. If he does this, let him possess the property.

III.

[If anyone flees to a church, let no one drag him forcibly from there.]

1. If any man pursues a fugitive, either a freeman or a slave, and he flees within the doors of a church, let no one have the authority to remove him from the church, but let him consider the honor of the church out of fear of God, and let him ask the priest of the church to speak on behalf of the slave to return him, and let him give a legitimate pledge so that the flight of the slave is pardoned. Then let the priest restore the slave to his master in peace.

2. If, however, the priest neglects or refuses to return the slave, let him keep [the slave] with him in the meantime, and take charge of him, so that the fugitive does not escape. And if he escapes, let the priest search for him without delay and restore him to his master; and if he cannot find him, let him restore another like him or pay his price.

[*If anyone drags a fugitive forcibly from a church.*]

3. If, however, a man removes [the fugitive] by force, thereby doing an injury to the church, let him pay thirty-six solidi to the church, and let him pay forty solidi as a *fredus* to the public treasury, since he went against the law, and did not consider the honor of the Church, and had no reverence for God. [Let this compensation be rendered] so others will know that the fear of God among Christians and the honor of the Church must be upheld.

IV.

[*If any freeman kills another freeman within a church.*]

If any freeman kills another freeman within the doors of a church, let him know that he acted unjustly against God and desecrated the church of God. To that church which he desecrated, let him pay forty solidi, and let him pay a *fredus* to the public treasury; however, to the relatives, let him pay a legitimate wergeld.

V.

[*If anyone forcibly removes entrusted property from a church.*]

1.[5] If anyone entrusts his property to a church and then someone removes it, and if this is done by theft, let the thief restore the property in full, and at whatever price those properties are valued, let him compensate for them ninefold. [If] he does this again, they are [to be compensated] thrice ninefold. All of this ought to be compensated to him whose property they are. Furthermore, let him pay thirty-six solidi to the church he dishonored.

2. If the thief removes this property from a church, and does this by force, let him compensate the owner doubly, in addition to twelve solidi. Nevertheless, let him give thirty-six solidi to the church as is stated above.

3. If a slave does this and does it at his master's command, let everything be observed as is stated above. If, however, a slave does this of his own accord, [the law] regarding theft ought to be observed as it is given; and if a slave does this through the use of force, let compensation not be exacted as in the case of a free-

man, but let the forcible act of the slave be compensated for, so that what he removed may simply be restored. If it is immediately discovered how this took place, it will not be regarded as an interference by his master. But if there was any delay, let twelve solidi be given because of the interference by his master. If his master is uninvolved in this thing, so that it was not done by his order, let four solidi be exacted from him as a *fredus*. For if it was at his order, let it be compensated as is stated above.

V a.[6]

Concerning oathtakers, of what sort and how many a man ought to have according to custom.

1. Concerning minor cases up to the value of a solidus, let it be permitted for anyone to have one oathtaker of any sort he wishes with him to swear his oath. But if a case arises concerning property valued at two saigae more than a solidus, then the man who initiates the case ought to name three chosen men, and of the three chosen men, the defendant has the right to reject two. However, he is not permitted to reject the third, but he must retain him for the oath.

2. However, a saiga is the fourth part of a tremissis, that is, one denarius.[7] Two saigae are two denarii. A tremissis is the third part of a solidus and is equal to four denarii.

3. Therefore, [the law] is to be observed up to three solidi. And if anyone is summoned [for property] appraised at two saigae more than three solidi, then let him who prosecutes the case make a choice of oathtakers from which the defendant has the right to reject two of whatever sort he wishes. And that regulation is to be observed with two oathtakers up to [the value of] six solidi. For if it is two more saigae, he ought to swear similarly with five chosen men, as it is stated above, with his own hand as a sixth. And in all these regulations, it is permitted to reject two chosen men.

4. Oaths ought to be sworn in which the oathtakers place their hands on a sacred object; and let the defendant alone, who represents the case, speak the appropriate words and place his hand above the hands of all, so that in this manner God may help him and those whose hands he covers, that he may not be found guilty in that case for which he is summoned.

VI.

[If anyone steals church property.]

If anyone steals property from a church and is convicted, so that he must pay for whatever property he stole, let him pay thrice ninefold, either for a slave or a maidservant, an ox, horse, or any animal whatever, or other property that belongs to a church. If the deed is discovered after the theft, let the doer pay as it is written above. If, however, he wishes to deny the deed, let him swear according to the value of the property with his oath-takers on the altar [of the church] from which the objects were stolen, [and let this be done] in the presence of a priest and his deacon whom the pastor of the church orders to hear the oath.

VII.

If anyone kills a slave of a church, let him compensate three-fold, and, as is accustomed for a slave of the king, let him pay forty-five solidi. And if he abducts him contrary to law and sells him outside the province, let him compensate threefold. And if anyone steals him, let him restore another of equal value, if he cannot find him. However, let him pay half his value in gold [and] half in any sort of property.

VIII.

[If anyone kills a freeman of (indentured to) a church.]

If, however, anyone kills a freeman of [indentured to] a church, whom they call a *colonus,* let him compensate as for other Alamans.

IX.

[If anyone armed enters the courtyard of a bishop.]

If anyone armed enters the courtyard of a bishop contrary to law, an act which the Alamans call [h]aisstera [h]anti, let him make a settlement of eighteen solidi. If he enters the house, let him pay thirty-six solidi.

X.

[If anyone enters the courtyard of a parish priest who is under the jurisdiction of a bishop.]

However, if anyone armed enters contrary to law into the courtyard of a priest who was placed in the parish by a bishop, let him return threefold compensation[8] to the priest, as is stated above, what other free Alamans are accustomed to be compensated.

XI.

[If anyone injures a bishop.]

If anyone injures, strikes, clubs, or cripples a bishop, let him make compensation on all things threefold what his relatives are rendered compensation. It is better if we say: let him settle with a bishop in every respect as with the duke. And if he kills him, let him pay just as for the duke, either to the king, the duke, or the church where he was pastor.

XII.

[If anyone injures a parish priest.]

If anyone, however, injures, clubs, cripples, or does any injury whatever to a parish priest, let him compensate threefold.[9] And if he kills him, let him compensate with 600 solidi for him, either to the church where he served or to the bishop in whose parish he was placed.

XIII.

[If anyone injures a deacon who is under the jurisdiction of a bishop.]

If anyone does any injury, or clubs, strikes, or cripples a deacon who reads the gospel in the presence of a bishop and performs his office before the altar in canonical robes, let him make a two-fold settlement. And if he kills him, let him pay 300 solidi.

XIV.

[If anyone injures a monk (who lives) by a rule.]

A monk, moreover, who takes a vow under a rule in a monastery and suffers some injury from another, [is to be compensated] similarly to a deacon as is stated above.

XV.

[Concerning the compensation of clerics.]

1. Clerics are to be compensated just as their relatives are.

[*Concerning the injury of clerics.*]

2. If a cleric, moreover, who publicly recites the liturgy from the pulpit of a church or sings the gradual[10] or hymn in the presence of a bishop, suffers an injury, as is described above, let him be compensated as his relatives are, and let a third part be added to this compensation.

XVI.

[*If anyone kills (a freeman) who was freed through a charter.*]

If freemen are killed who were manumitted in a church or who received their freedom through a charter, let eighty solidi be paid to the church or to their [the freemen's] sons.

XVII.

[*If any freewoman marries a slave.*]

1. Concerning maidservants. If a freewoman was manumitted by a charter or in a church, and after this she married a slave, let her remain permanently a maidservant of the church.

2. If, however, a free Alamannic woman marries a church slave and refuses the servile work of a maidservant, let her depart. If, however, she gives birth to sons or daughters there, let them remain slaves and maidservants permanently, and let them not have the right of departure. However, the mother of these children, when she wishes to depart, has the right for three years. If, however, she performs the work of a maidservant for three years and her relatives have not redeemed her in order that she may become free, either before the duke or a count, or in the public assembly with the passing of three meetings of the Marchfield,[11] then let her always remain a maidservant, and let those who are born of her be slaves and maidservants.

XVIII.

[*If anyone (attempts) to obtain possession of church property without a charter.*]

Let no layman attempt to obtain possession of church property without a charter, and if he does not produce a charter, which he can acquire from the priest of a church, let possession always remain with the church.

XIX.

[Let no one sell church property.]

Let no priest or any pastor of a church have the right to sell church land unless in exchange for other land, [not even] a slave [*mancipium*]¹² unless he receives another slave. And if he makes a bargain concerning the slave or the land, let him always confirm it through a letter, so that there is no dispute and the church may not lose what it ought to possess lawfully.

XX.

[If anyone receives a church slave as a fugitive.]

If anyone receives an agricultural slave [*mancipium,* that is, a slave indentured to a manor] or a [domestic ?] slave or maid-servant of a church as a fugitive, and after either the priest himself or a legitimate messenger inquires, he neglects to return him and opposes the law, let him pay threefold the amount customarily given in compensation to other Alamans. And whatever he does to a church contrary to law, let him compensate all things threefold, as the law requires.

XXI.

[Let slaves of the church render their tribute.]

Church slaves should render as their lawful tribute the following: fifteen measures of beer, a pig worth one tremissis, two bushels of bread, five chickens, [and] twenty eggs. Maidservants, however, should do their servile work without neglect. Let slaves keep half the crops for themselves and render half to their masters. And if there is more work, let the ecclesiastical slaves work three days for their masters and three days for themselves.

XXII.

[Let church freemen (coloni) *render tribute just as* (freemen) *of the king do.]*

1. However, concerning ecclesiastical freemen, whom they call *coloni,* let them render all things to a church just as the *coloni* of the king do. If anyone refuses to pay lawful tribute ordered by his judge, let him be liable for six solidi. And if he does not fulfill

the work that is required of him in the manner the law requires, let him owe six solidi.

2. And if a judge, by order of his lord, sends any seal or mark of any sort and orders a man to come or go for any purpose, and that man neglects it, let him be liable for six solidi. If, however, he ignores the bishop's seal, or neglects to come or go where ordered, let him be liable for twelve solidi.

XXIII.

[If anyone conspires to take the duke's life.]

Concerning cases which pertain to the duke.[13]

If any man conspires to take the duke's life and is convicted thereafter, either let him lose his life or redeem himself as the duke or popular princes judge. And if he wishes to swear, let him swear in a church with twelve designated men before the duke or before one whom the duke sends.

XXIV.

[If anyone invites a foreign nation into the province.]

If any man invites a foreign nation into the province, so that it is plundered in a hostile manner or houses are burned, and he is convicted of this, let him either lose his life or go into exile where the duke sends him, and let his property be confiscated by the state.

XXV.

[If anyone stirs up a quarrel within the army.]

1. Concerning those who stir up a quarrel within the army so that in the uproar people clash using arms, and a fight arises within their own army, and someone is killed there: let that man who began this either lose his life or go into exile, and let his property be confiscated by the state.

2. And let those others who accompanied him there or participated pay threefold, as the law requires.

XXVI.

[If anyone steals from the army.]

1. If anyone steals something from the army, when the king leads the army, let him pay nine times ninefold for whatever he stole.

2. If, however, the duke leads the army and someone steals something from the public treasury, let him pay thrice ninefold. And if he wishes to swear, let him swear according to the value of the property.

XXVII.

[If anyone neglects the seal or order of his duke.]

1. If anyone neglects the duke's seal or any order or sign that he sends, let him be liable for twelve solidi. And if he wishes to deny that the messenger came to him, let him swear with five designated men, if his lord wishes to offer an oath to him.

2. If, however, he disregards the seal or order of a count, let him compensate with six solidi.

3. If, however, he disregards the seal or order of a hundred-man,[14] let him be liable for three solidi. And if he wishes to deny that the messenger came to him, let him swear according to what he ought to pay.

XXVIII.

[If anyone kills a man in the duke's courtyard.]

1. If anyone kills a man in the duke's courtyard or going to or returning from there, let him pay a triple wergeld since he violated the duke's command, so that every man may have peace coming to his lord or returning from him.

2. Let no one attempt to inhibit a man on a journey coming from the duke or going to him, even if he is guilty. And if one attempts to do something to him or kills him, whether the man escapes alive or is injured, let the perpetrator always compensate for him threefold.

3. And if he goes to a count and is killed there or injured, let him who did this compensate for all things threefold.

XXIX.

[If anyone kills the duke's messenger.]

If anyone kills the duke's messenger within the province, let him pay threefold for him, as the law requires. If he wishes to deny that he did this, let him swear as the law requires, with twelve designated men and twelve other chosen men.

XXX.

[If anyone steals something within the king's courtyard.]

If anyone steals from someone in the king's courtyard, let him compensate twofold to him from whom he stole, and let him pay forty solidi as a *fredus* to the state. If another's slave does this in the duke's courtyard, let his master redeem him for what he is worth or give him up.

XXXI.

[If anyone steals the duke's property.]

If anyone steals from the duke something that belongs to him [the duke], thereafter let him compensate thrice ninefold, and let him not render a *fredus,* since these are manorial properties and are compensated threefold.

XXXII.

[Concerning women who are in the duke's service.]

If anyone does something contrary to law to women who are in the duke's service, let him compensate for all things three times what other Alamannic [women] are compensated.

XXXIII.

If anyone starts a fight in the duke's courtyard, and a quarrel arises there, and through his action people clash, whatever is done there through his action, let the man [who started the fight] compensate threefold for what he disregards and what he does contrary to law. However, let him through whose voice or act this dispute arose compensate with sixty[15] solidi to the state.

XXXIV.

[*If anyone takes ducal property in a hostile way.*]

1. If anyone attempts to intrude on ducal possessions in a hostile way and plunders them, and he is convicted, let him restore threefold whatever he plundered there, [either] slaves [or] money, and, moreover, let him pay his wergeld to the duke, since he acted contrary to law.

2. And however many freemen follow him there as thieves and are convicted thereafter, let each forfeit sixty solidi to the duke and restore threefold whatever they removed from there.

XXXV.

[*Concerning the (duke's) son who rebels against his father.*]

1. If any duke has an insolent and evil son who attempts to rebel against his father, through his own folly or because of the advice of evil men who wish to disrupt the province, and if he rises against his father forcibly while his father is still able to serve the king and lead the army, mount a horse, [and] fulfill service to the king, and his son wishes to dishonor him or possess his dukedom through thievery, let him not complete what he started. And if the father is able to conquer and capture him, then let it be in his [father's] power either to exile him from the province or to send him wherever he wishes, even to the king his lord, and let nothing of the paternal inheritance belong to him, since he committed an unlawful act against his father.

2. And if he has brothers, let these brothers divide the father's inheritance among themselves according to the will of the king; however, to him who rebelled against his father, let them give him no portion. If there is no other son than the one who rebelled, then let the ducal inheritance be in the power of the king to give to whomever he wishes, or even to the very son of the duke who rebelled, if he can obtain this by serving the king. If the king wishes to give it to another, then let it be in his power to do so.

XXXVI.

[*Let the court take place (according) to ancient custom.*]

1. The court shall take place according to ancient custom in every hundred[16] in the presence of the count or his representative

and in the presence of the hundred-man.[17] The juridical assembly[18] should take place every Saturday[19] or on such a day as the count or hundred-man wishes, that is, once a week[20] when there is little peace in the province. However, when times are better, the assembly should take place every two weeks in every hundred, as we said above.

2. And if anyone wishes to summon another for any dispute whatever, he ought to summon him publicly before his judge so the judge may restrain him according to law, and let him render justice to his neighbor, no matter who wishes to summon him. First, let him present his dispute before the assembly. Second, if he wishes to swear, let him swear according to the established law. And in the first meeting of the assembly, let him respond with an oathtaker and give witnesses as the law requires, and let him give his pledge to the representative of the count or to that hundred-man who is present, so that he may swear lawfully on the established day. If he is liable, let him compensate so that he does not fail to come through neglect, and if he fails to come, let him always be liable for sixty solidi as a *fredus*. However, let [no one] restrain him, so that neglect does not occur, neither let the poor suffer injury, nor be without law, nor curse the duke or the people of the land. But let there be order in all things, so that those who rebel may be restrained from evil actions and those who are good may possess the peace.

3. If any freeman, however, refuses to come to that assembly or does not present himself to the count, the hundred-man, or the representative of the count in the assembly, let him be liable for twelve solidi. Let no person whatever refuse to come to the assembly, neither a vassal of the duke or the count nor any person whatever, so that in the assembly the poor may present their cases. And let what cannot be finished in one assembly be finished in another, so that the land may be defended free from the wrath of God, and those rebels who cause disruption of whatever kind may no longer have the power of doing so. And if there is such a person whom the count, the hundred-man, or the representative of the count cannot restrain in the assembly, then let the duke restrain him lawfully. Seek to please God rather than man, so that no negligence may be found in the duke's soul by God.

XXXVII.

[Let no one sell slaves outside the province.]

1. Let no one sell slaves [*mancipia*] outside the province, whether among pagans or Christians, unless it is done by the order of the duke.

2. Within the province, when it is necessary, let each man have the power of deciding [the fate] of his slave according to law. However, let him not have the power of holding him in captivity outside the province. If, however, anyone does this and thereafter is convicted according to our decree that applies to all Alamans, and if anyone wishes to transgress this order, let him lose the price he assigned to his own slave, and, in addition, let him make compensation of a *fredus,* which the law requires.

XXXVIII.

[Let Sunday be celebrated.]

Let no one attempt to perform servile work on Sunday, since the law prohibits this and Holy Scripture has pronounced against it in every way. If any slave is found guilty of this offense, let him be beaten with sticks. However, let a freeman be corrected up to the third time. If, however, after the third warning he is found guilty of this offense, and refuses to serve God on Sunday, and does servile work, then let him lose a third part of his inheritance. If, however, after this it is found that he did not render honor on Sunday and did servile work, [and] then he is arrested and convicted before the count, then let him be pressed into slavery where the duke orders. Since he did not serve God, let him always remain a slave.

XXXIX.

[Concerning incestuous marriages.]

We prohibit incestuous marriages. Accordingly, it is not permitted to have as wife a mother-in-law, daughter-in-law, step-daughter, step-mother, brother's daughter, sister's daughter, brother's wife, or wife's sister. Brother's children and sister's children are under no pretext to be joined together. If anyone acts against this, let them [the married pair] be separated by the judges in that place, and let them lose all their property, which the public treasury shall acquire. If there are lesser persons who pollute themselves through an illicit union, let them lose their freedom; let them be added to the public slaves.

XL.

[*If anyone wishes to kill his parents.*]

Concerning parricide [*and*] *fratricide.*[21]

If any man willingly kills his father, his brother, his uncle, his brother's son, his mother, or his sister, let him know that he acted against God, and, since he was not his brother's keeper according to God's commandment, that he seriously sinned against God. And in the presence of all his relatives, let his property be confiscated and let nothing more descend to his heirs. However, let him receive punishment according to the canons of the Church.

XLI.

[*Let a judge decide disputes.*]

1. Let no one attempt to hear disputes unless he is appointed as a judge by the duke through agreement with the people to judge disputes, and is neither a liar, a perjurer, nor a receiver of gifts; but let him judge disputes truthfully according to law regardless of person, and let him fear God. And if he judges justly, let him believe that he is to receive reward from God and possess high praise from men. If, however, he judges contrary to law through greed, envy of someone, or fear, let him know that he has sinned, and let him be liable for twelve solidi to him whom he judged unjustly, and let the judge restore to him what he has suffered unjustly through that loss.

2. Now if he who should hear a judgment despises the judgment rendered in this matter, when the judge has adjudicated justly, and he refuses to hear him, and abuses him, and argues before the others, and says, "You have not judged justly," (though he [the judge] did judge justly), and if this is investigated by other judges who affirm that he [the judge] judged justly, let the despiser, who does an injury to the judge, pay twelve solidi to that judge. And after this, let him not despise to hear a just judgment, since the duke and all the people have decided in favor of it in the public assembly.

XLII.

[Concerning true and false witnesses.]

1. If anyone is questioned before the duke regarding any dispute whatever, concerning either a homicide, a theft, or some neglect, which is now made evident by three or four witnesses, let those who testify be good witnesses among the people, not perjurers, imposers, or receivers of gifts, but persons wishing to speak the truth. Let the judge know this. Then that man has no permission or power to swear in court before the judge concerning the dispute, but, as the law requires, let him abide by this judgment, so that from this crime others who wish God's will may not perjure themselves, or suffer loss through another's fault. In addition, let no witness who is proven to have testified falsely once, or twice, or three times, be received any more in testimony.

[Concerning validating documents.]

2. A written document is not valid unless on it the year and the day are clearly indicated.

XLIII.

[If anyone incriminates another in the presence of the king.]

If any freeman attributes a capital crime to another freeman, and accuses him before the king or duke, and thereafter it is not proven apart from what he himself claims, let the accused be permitted to clear himself with a drawn sword against the other who incriminated him. However, let minor offenses between [contending parties] be settled as the duke wishes.

XLIV.

[If anyone kills another in the street.]

*Concerning disputes that commonly occur
among the people.*[22]

1. If any dispute arises between two men, either in the street or the field, and one kills the other, and afterwards he who killed him flees, and his peers follow him into his house with weapons and kill the murderer inside his house, let him [the second] be paid for[23] with a single wergeld.

2. If, however, they remain over his corpse in the field where the fight first started and do not follow [the murderer] into his house, and afterwards they go into the neighborhood, assemble their peers, put aside their weapons, and then follow him into his house in a hostile way and kill him, let him be paid for[24] by a ninefold wergeld.

XLV.

[*If anyone sells a freeman outside the borders.*]

If any freeman sells another freeman outside the borders, let him bring him back into the province, restore his freedom to him, and compensate with forty solidi. If, however, he cannot bring him back, let him pay for him with the wergeld to his relatives—if he has an heir—that is, twice eighty solidi. If, however, he has no heir, let him compensate with 200 solidi.

XLVI.

[*If anyone sells a freewoman outside the borders* (marca).]

If, however, anyone sells a freewoman outside the borders [*marcha*], let him restore her former freedom to her and compensate with eighty solidi. If, however, he cannot bring her back, let him compensate with 400 solidi.

XLVII.

[*If anyone sells a freeman within the province.*]

If a freeman sells another freeman within the province, let him restore his former freedom to him and compensate with twelve solidi. If, however, he sells a freewoman within the province, let him restore her former freedom to her and compensate with twenty-four solidi.

XLVIII.

[*If anyone kills a man.*]

If anyone murders another, which the Alamans call *mortaudo*,[25] let him pay a ninefold wergeld for him and compensate for whatever weapons and clothing he stole from him, as if it were done in secret. If, however, this happens to women, let that man compensate twofold.²⁶ Let him compensate for the clothing she wore as if he stole in secret.

XLIX.

[If anyone exhumes a freeman from the ground.]

1. If anyone exhumes a freeman from the ground, let him restore whatever he stole there with a ninefold wergeld and compensate with forty solidi. If, however, he exhumes a woman from the ground, let him compensate with eighty solidi. Let him compensate for the property he stole [as if he stole] in secret.

2. If he exhumes a slave from the ground, let him compensate with twelve solidi; and a maidservant similarly.

L.

[If anyone abducts another's wife.]

1. If any freeman abducts another's wife contrary to law, let him return her and compensate with eighty solidi. If, however, he does not wish to return her, let him pay for her with 400 solidi, if the previous husband agrees to receive this payment.²⁷ And if she dies before her husband sought her, let him [the abductor] compensate with 400 solidi.

2. If, however, that abductor, who took her for himself as a wife, has sons and daughters by her before he pays for her, and a son or daughter dies, let him pay for that child to the former husband with the wergeld. If, however, the children are living, they do not belong to him who begot them, but remain under the guardianship [*mundium*] of the former husband.

LI.

[If anyone takes another's betrothed.]

If anyone takes another's betrothed contrary to law, let him return her and compensate with 200 solidi. If, however, he does not wish to return her, let him pay for her with 400 solidi, even if she dies under his [custody].²⁸

LII.

[If anyone dismisses another's betrothed daughter.]

If anyone dismisses another's betrothed daughter and takes another, let him compensate for her whom he betrothed and dismissed with forty solidi, and let him swear with twelve oathtakers, five designated and six selected [himself as the twelfth], that he rejects her through no vice or contempt, nor does he find any fault in her, but love of another led him to dismiss her and take another as a wife.

LIII.

[*If anyone takes an unbetrothed daughter.*]

1. If anyone takes another's unbetrothed daughter for himself as a wife, let him return her and compensate for her with forty solidi, if her father demands her back.[29]

2. If, however, this woman dies under his [custody], before he acquired the guardianship [*mundium*] from her father, let him pay 400 solidi for her to her father. And if he begets sons and daughters before [he acquires the *mundium*], and all their children die, let him compensate to the woman's father with the wergeld for each child.

LIV.

[*If anyone dies without heirs.*]

1. If any freeman dies leaving a wife without sons or daughters and she wishes to give up the inheritance to marry another of equal status to her own, let a lawful dowry accompany her, and whatever his relatives lawfully give her and whatever she took with her from her father's inheritance, let her have the right of taking with her all the things that she has not consumed or sold. In addition, a lawful dowry consists of 400 solidi, either in gold, silver, slaves, or whatever other property he gave.[30]

[*If the nearest relative refuses a dowry to the wife of a deceased husband.*]

2. If, however, the nearest relative of the deceased husband wishes to refuse a dowry to that woman, which is illegal, let him [the relative who refused] take an oath with five designated men or with wager of battle between two fighters with drawn swords. If she [the widow] can acquire the property either through an oath or through combat, let that property never revert back after the death of the woman, but let her next husband or his children possess it forever.

3. If, however, that woman says: "My husband gave a *mor-gangeba*[31] [morning gift] to me," let her estimate its worth, either in gold, silver, slaves, or horses, estimating the property at twelve solidi. Then let it be permitted to that woman to swear on her heart and say: "My husband gave this property to me under my own jurisdiction, and I should possess it." This the Alamans call *nasthait*.

LV.

[*If two sisters survive their father's death.*]

If, moreover, two sisters are left after the death of their father without a brother, and the paternal inheritance belongs to them, and one marries a freeman of equal status to herself, whereas the other marries a *colonus* of the king or a *colonus* of a church, let her who marries a freeman of equal status to herself inherit the land of their father; however, let them divide other property equally. Let her who marries the *colonus* not receive a portion of the land, since she did not marry [a man] of equal status to herself.

LVI.

[*If anyone uncovers a woman's head.*]

1. If any free virgin woman [maiden] goes on a journey between two estates, and anyone meets her [and] uncovers her head, let him compensate with six[32] solidi. And if he raises her clothing to the knee, let him compensate with six solidi. And if he exposes her so that her genitalia or posterior appears, let him compensate with twelve solidi. If, however, he fornicates with her against her will, let him compensate with forty solidi.

2. If, however, this happens to an adult woman, let him compensate all things twice what we said above concerning the virgin.

LVII.

[*If anyone strikes another through anger, (called) pulislac.*]

1. If anyone strikes another through anger, which the Alamans call *pulislac,* let him compensate with one solidus.

2. If, however, he draws blood so that it drips on the ground, let him compensate with one and one-half solidi.

3. But if he strikes him so that the skull appears and is scratched, let him compensate with three solidi.

4. If, however, a bone of the head is broken away by a blow, so that the bone [when thrown] sounds against a shield from a distance of twenty-four feet on a public road, let him compensate with six solidi.

5. If, however, a physician loses that bone and cannot present it, then let him call two witnesses who have seen that the bone broke away by that blow, or let that physician prove that the bone broke away by that blow.

6. If, however, the skull is cut through so that the brain appears and a physician can touch it with a feather or a cloth, let him compensate with twelve solidi.

7. If, however, the brain protrudes from the wound, as often happens, so that a physician mends [the skull] with medication or silk and afterwards [the patient] recovers, and this is proved to be true, let him [the giver of the blow] compensate with forty solidi.

[*Concerning the cutting off of another's ear and arm.*]

8. If anyone cuts off another's ear and it does not make him deaf, let him compensate with twelve solidi.

9. If, however, he cuts deeply and it makes him deaf, let him compensate with forty solidi.

10. Furthermore, if he cuts off half the ear, which the Alamans call *scardi,* let him compensate with six solidi.

11. Furthermore, if he mutilates the upper eyelid so that it cannot be closed, let him compensate with six solidi.

12. Furthermore, if he mutilates the lower [eyelid] so that it cannot contain tears, let him compensate with twelve solidi.

13. Furthermore, if the sight of the eye is impaired so that [the eye] remains glassy, let him compensate with twenty solidi.

14. If, however, the eye protrudes, let him compensate with forty solidi.

15. Furthermore, if the nose is pierced, let him compensate with six solidi.

16. Furthermore, if the top of the nose is cut off so that it cannot contain mucus, let him compensate with twelve solidi.

17. If, however, the entire [nose] to the base is cut off, let him compensate with forty solidi.

18. Moreover, if he mutilates the upper lip of another so that the teeth appear, let him compensate with six solidi.

19. And for the lower [lip] so that it cannot contain saliva, let him compensate with twelve solidi.

20. But if anyone knocks out another's two upper front teeth with a blow, let him compensate with six solidi.

21. And if he knocks out one of these two, let him compensate with six solidi.

22. If, however, he knocks out the tooth which the Alamans call *marczan,* let him compensate with three solidi.

23. [If] he knocks out other [teeth] of whatever kind, let him compensate for each with one solidus.

24. [If] he knocks out another's two lower front [teeth], let him compensate with twelve solidi, if he does this with one blow.

25. If, however, he knocks out one of these, let him compensate with twelve solidi.

26. If, moreover, the entire tongue is cut off, let him compensate with forty solidi. If, however, half [the tongue is cut off] so that he is intelligible when he speaks, let him compensate with twenty solidi.

27. If, however, any blow strikes someone in the face so that the hair or the beard does not grow, let him compensate with six solidi.

28. If, moreover, the neck is pierced, let him compensate with six solidi.

29. If anyone accidentally strikes the head of another freeman contrary to law, let him compensate with twelve solidi.

30. But if he accidentally strikes someone's beard, let him compensate with six solidi.

31. If anyone pierces another's arm above the elbow, let him compensate with six solidi.

32. If, however, he pierces [below][33] the elbow, let him compensate with three solidi.

33. If he pierces the hand so that a cauterizing iron is not applied to the veins, and stops the bleeding, let him compensate with one and one-half solidi.

34. If, however, a cauterizing iron is applied to stop the bleeding, let him compensate with three solidi.

35. But if he breaks the arm below the elbow so that he does

not break the skin, which the Alamans call *balebrust,* let him compensate with three solidi.

36. If, however, this happens above the knee, let him compensate with six solidi.

37. But if he strikes an elbow so that he cannot carry anything or move his hand to his mouth, let him compensate with twelve solidi.

38. But if an entire arm is crippled so that he cannot do anything with it, let him compensate him with twenty solidi.

[*Concerning the cutting off of the arm.*]

39. If, however, he cuts off [an arm] from the elbow, let him compensate with forty solidi.

40. If, however, [an arm] is cut off from the shoulder, let him compensate with eighty solidi.

[*Concerning the cutting off of the hand and finger.*]

41. But if he cuts off the top of the thumb, let him compensate with six solidi.

42. If, however, an entire [thumb, let him compensate] with twelve solidi.

43. If, however, he cuts off a forefinger at the first joint, let him compensate with two and one-half solidi.

44. But if he cuts off [a forefinger] at the second joint, [let him compensate with] five solidi.

45. If he cuts off [a forefinger] from the palm, let him compensate with ten solidi.

46. If a middle finger is cut off at the first joint, let him compensate with one and one-half solidi.

47. If at the second joint, [let him compensate with] three solidi.

48. If an entire [middle finger] is cut off from the palm, let him compensate with six solidi.

49. But if a ring finger is cut off at the first joint, let him compensate with two solidi.

50. If at the second joint, [let him compensate with] four solidi.

51. If an entire [ring finger, let him compensate with] eight solidi.

52. A little finger is to be paid for equal to the thumb.

53. If, however, anyone injures a middle finger so that thereafter it is crippled, and it cannot be bent, or grasp a shield, or pick up weapons from the ground, let him compensate with twelve solidi.

[*Concerning the piercing of the side.*]

54. If, moreover, a man is pierced in the side so that he cannot retain the internal organs, let him [the doer] compensate with six solidi.

55. If, however, the internal organs are injured, which they call *hrevovunt,* let him compensate with twelve solidi.

56. If he pierces them, let him compensate with twenty-four solidi.

57. If, however, he mutilates the intestines so that the excrement comes out, let him compensate with forty solidi.

58. If anyone cuts off the entire genitalia of another, let him compensate with forty solidi.

59. If, however, he castrates him so that he loses his virility, let him compensate with twenty solidi.

[*Concerning hips, knees, and legs.*]

60. If anyone pierces both hips of another with one thrust, let him compensate with twelve solidi.

61. If with two thrusts, [let him compensate] similarly.

62. If, however, one injures another in the knee so that he remains lame and his foot drags on the ground [literally, through the dew], which the Alamans call *tautragil,* let him compensate with twelve solidi.

63. If a leg is pierced below the knee, let him compensate with three solidi.

[*Concerning the cutting off of feet and toes.*]

64. If, however, a big toe is cut off, let him [the doer] compensate with six solidi.

65. If all other toes are cut off, let him compensate each with three solidi.

66. If he cuts off an entire foot, let him compensate with forty solidi.

[*Concerning the knee again and a hernia.*]

67. If [a leg] is cut off at the knee, let him compensate with fifty solidi.

68. If [an entire leg] is cut off from the hip, and he lives thereafter, let him compensate with eighty solidi.

69. If, however, anyone causes a hernia in another, let him compensate with three solidi.

LVIII.

[*If anyone blocks another's way.*]

If any freeman raises his hand in the way of another freeman and blocks his way contrary to law, or wishes to take something from him, let him compensate with six solidi.

LIX.

[*If anyone throws another from his horse on the road.*]

1. If any freeman throws another freeman from his horse on the road, and takes the horse but immediately returns it to that place, let him add one similar to it and twelve solidi.

2. Let all this compensation that we have determined for men be rendered twofold to their women.

LX.

[*If any freeman kills another freeman.*]

1. If, however, any freeman kills another freeman, let him compensate for him with twice eighty solidi to his children. If, however, he leaves no children and has no relatives, let him [the killer] pay 200 solidi for him.

2. Women, however, [are] always [to be compensated] twofold.

3. If an ordinary Alaman is killed, let him [the killer] pay 200 solidi for him to his relatives.

LXI.

[*Concerning the stealing of a stallion.*]

1. If anyone steals another's stallion, he to whom [it belongs] must prove what it is worth. But if he says that it is worth twelve solidi, let him swear with two men that it is worth that much, and then let the thief pay him as much as he swore to personally, and

let him [the thief] pay an eightfold wergeld for it, half in gold, and half in whatever property he can find.

2. And if he steals such a horse as the Alamans call *marach,* let him pay for it just as for that stallion.

LXII.

[Concerning the stealing of another's horse.]

1. If anyone steals another's horse, let its owner appraise it up to six solidi with an oath. Let him appraise it up to the value of six solidi, but let him not seek more; let him value it neither more nor less. At whatever it is appraised under oath in his presence, let the thief restore that much. Moreover, [let him pay] an eightfold wergeld in whatever money he has.

2. Let him appraise a draft horse at three solidi, whether it is worth that much or less.

LXIII.

[If anyone knocks out an eye of the horse (known as) marach.]

1. If a man knocks out an eye or cuts off the tail of the horse they call *marach,* let him compensate with three solidi.

2. If he knocks out the eye of another's horse, [an animal] of average value, let him compensate with one and one-half solidi; and if he cuts off its tail, let him compensate similarly.

3. But if he knocks out the eye of a draft horse, let him compensate with one-half solidus; and if he cuts off its tail, let him compensate similarly.

LXIV.

[If anyone injures a horse while its owner sits on it.]

If a man is riding his horse and anyone wishes to injure him while he is on it and injures the horse instead when the assailant strikes at him, let him make compensation for the horse as if he did this to the owner.

LXV.

[If anyone steals a lead horse from (a troop) of draft horses.]

1. But if anyone steals the lead horse from a troop of draft horses, let its owner be permitted to appraise it at twelve solidi.

And whatever he appraises it at, let that thief restore that theft ninefold.

2. However, for the draft horses of the herd that are milk-giving, let him compensate with six solidi.

3. However, let other horses that are not pregnant at that time be appraised at three solidi.

LXVI.

[If anyone causes an abortion (in a horse) by a blow.]

If, however, any man strikes a pregnant draft horse with a blow and causes an abortion so that the colt comes forth dead, let him compensate with one solidus.

LXVII.

[If anyone offers a herd of draft horses as a pledge.]

1. If anyone offers a herd of draft horses as a pledge and encloses them unlawfully, let him compensate with twelve solidi and return them, and let him who has them as a pledge maintain them in his custody for an entire year. And if he loses any of the herd in that year, let him who offers the pledge always replace each horse with one equal in value.

2. If, however, that herd of draft horses does damage either in the meadow or among the crops, let them be driven out, and let their owner come to see what damage is done. And for the estimated amount or for as much damage as they have done, which you have affirmed,[34] let the owner of the herd restore that much.

3. If anyone kills the herdsman of that herd, let him compensate with forty solidi.

LXVIII.

[If anyone steals or kills a bull.]

1. If anyone steals or kills a bull from a lawful herd where there are twelve or more cows, let him pay three solidi for it. For whatever animal of that herd he steals, let him pay according to its value.

2. It is permitted to appraise that best cow at four tremisses.

3. [Let] the cow that comes next [in value be appraised] at one solidus.

4. Let those animals of little value, which are appraised at an estimated amount, be paid for as the law requires.

LXIX.

[Concerning the wergeld of a murdered man or woman.]

If anyone murders [*mortaudus fuerit*] a man [*baro*] or a woman who is [free], let a lawful wergeld be paid ninefold, or let the doer swear with twenty-four men, all chosen, or with eighty, whomever he can find.

Pactus XV.

LXX.

[If anyone bewitches a pregnant woman.]

If any woman is pregnant and through the act of another the child is born dead, or if it is born alive but does not live for nine[35] nights, let him who is accused pay forty solidi or swear with twelve men, half of whom are chosen.

Pactus XII.

LXXI.

[Concerning the price of an ox.]

1. The best ox is worth five tremisses.
2. An average ox is worth four tremisses.
3. For less valuable oxen, let their worth be what they are appraised.
4. Let him who steals one of these pay as the law requires.

LXXII.

[If anyone kills a swineherd.]

Concerning a swineherd.[36]

If any swineherd is killed who has forty pigs in his herd and a trained dog, a horn, and a young helper, let the perpetrator compensate with forty solidi.

LXXIII.

If a lawful shepherd is killed who has eighty head in his master's flock, let the perpetrator compensate with forty solidi.

LXXIV.

1. If someone's steward is killed who is a slave and whose lord has twelve domestic retainers, let the perpetrator compensate with forty solidi.

2. If someone's marshal is killed who oversees twelve horses, let the perpetrator compensate with forty solidi.

3. If a cook is killed who has a young helper, let the perpetrator compensate with forty solidi.

4. If a baker [is killed, let the perpetrator compensate] similarly.

5. If a blacksmith, a goldsmith, or a swordmaker who is publicly attested is killed, let the perpetrator compensate with forty solidi for each.

LXXV.

[If anyone violates another's chambermaid.]

1. If anyone lies with someone's chambermaid against her will, let him compensate with six solidi.

2. And if anyone lies with the first maid of the textile workshop against her will, let him compensate with six solidi.

3. If anyone lies with other maids of the textile workshop against their will, let him compensate with three solidi.

LXXVI.

[If anyone sets another's house on fire at night.]

1. If anyone sets another's property on fire at night so that he burns his house and his home, and it is discovered and proven, let him restore what he burnt with equal value, and, in addition to this, let him compensate with forty solidi.

2. But if he burns a building within the courtyard, either a storehouse, a granary, or a provision house, let him restore everything with equal value and compensate with twelve solidi.

LXXVII.

1. If anyone burns an oven, a sheepfold, or a pigsty, let him compensate each with three solidi and restore one equal in value.

2. If he burns the house of a slave, let him compensate with twelve solidi and restore one equal in value.

3. If he burns a storehouse of a slave, let him compensate with six solidi and restore one equal in value.

4. But if he burns a granary of a slave, let him compensate with three solidi, and if a lord's, [let him compensate] with six solidi and restore one equal in value.

LXXVIII.

[Concerning the stealing of hunting dogs.]

Concerning hunting dogs.[37]

1. [If] a man steals [a hunting dog] that runs first, let him compensate with six solidi.

2. For that which runs second, let him compensate with three solidi.

3. Let him who steals a lead dog (that leads a man), which they call *laitihunt,* compensate with twelve solidi.

4. If anyone kills a good pig dog, a bear dog, or one that guards a cow or bull, let him compensate with three solidi. Or if he kills a trained greyhound, let him compensate with three solidi.

5. If anyone kills a sheep dog that kills wolves, and pulls the calf from its mouth, and runs barking to one estate or another, let him compensate with three solidi.

6. If anyone kills a dog that defends someone's courtyard, let him compensate with one solidus. And if that dog seizes him by the clothing, and he unwillingly strikes it, and it is killed, let him swear that he did not do it with malice but in self-defense, [and] let him give another puppy [that is grown enough] to wear a collar.

LXXIX.

[Concerning the building of a dam in water.]

If anyone builds a dam in water and the water overflows, and [if] someone's cow, slave, or child is killed there, let him make restoration of equal value. For each, let him compensate according to the law.[38]

LXXX.

[*Concerning a mill (or any) dam in water.*]

If anyone wishes to build a mill or any dam in water, let him do this [if] he injures no one. If, however, he injures someone, let him break it apart so that it causes no further injury. If both banks are his, he may have permission [to build it]; if however one bank is another's, let him ask permission.

LXXXI.

[*If a dispute arises between kindred.*]

If any dispute arises between two kinsmen concerning the boundaries of their land, [and] one says: "This is our boundary," [and] the other goes over to another place and says: "This is our boundary," let the count of that district, when he is present, put up a sign where the former wishes the boundary to be and one where the other wishes the boundary to be, and let them present the dispute. After it is presented, let them meet and in the presence of the count pick up [a clod] of earth, which the Alamans call *corfo,* and let them stick branches from trees into the earth that they picked up,[39] and let the kindred who are quarreling lift up that [clod] of earth in the presence of the count and commend it into his hand. Let him [the count] wrap it in a cloth, put his seal on it, and commend it into a trustworthy hand, according to established custom. Then let them respond with wager of battle among themselves. When they are preparing for the duel, let them place [the clod] of earth between them and touch this with the swords with which they are going to fight, and let them call God the Creator to witness, so that God may give victory to him who has a just claim; and let them fight. Let him who conquers among them win the dispute, and let those others compensate with twelve solidi, since they opposed the owner.

LXXXII.

[*If anyone receives a fugitive and does not wish to restore him to his master.*]

If anyone receives another's fugitive slave and does not wish to restore him to his pursuing master, either on that day or subsequently, [and] he detains him, then let him go to his chief leader, whomever he has, so that this man may render him justice. And let him compensate with twelve[40] solidi, since he received him [the fugitive] contrary to law.

LXXXIII.

[Concerning injurious pledges.]

1. If anyone contrary to law takes either a slave or a horse as a pledge [and] after he [the pledgee] brings the slave to his house, the slave kills a man there, or the horse does any damage, let the responsibility be borne by him who took the pledge, rather than by him whose pledge it was.

2. If, however, someone willingly gives a pledge to another for any property, and the pledge that was given does some damage there, let the pledger who gave it restore equally for the loss that occurred.

LXXXIV.

[If anyone (refuses to return) another's property.]

If anyone finds his property with another man, whatever it is, either slaves, cattle, gold, silver, or other stolen property, and if the latter does not wish to return it and resists this, and afterwards is convicted of this before a judge, let the perpetrator return property equal in value, or the same property, and compensate with twelve solidi, since he opposed the owner.

LXXXV.

[Do not let one brother dissipate another brother's property before they divide (the paternal inheritance).]

If any brothers receive an inheritance after the death of their father, let them divide their father's portion. When this is not yet done, let no one dissipate the [late father's] property before it is equally divided [among the late father's children].

LXXXVI.

[Concerning swearing for homicide.]

1. If anyone kills a man and wishes to deny it, let him swear with eleven designated men and as many other selected men summoned to swear on their consecrated weapons.

2. For [property valued at] four tremisses, let him swear with one oathtaker.

3. For [property valued at] three solidi and a tremissis, let him swear with two oathtakers.

4. For [property valued at] six solidi and a tremissis, let him swear with five selected men, or let him defend himself with a drawn sword.

LXXXVII.

[Concerning the cutting off (of the leg) at the knee.]

1. If a leg of a freeman is cut off, let him [the doer] compensate with eighty solidi.[41]

2. If an arm is cut off from the shoulder, let him pay similarly.[42]

LXXXVIII.

[Concerning an abortion in a woman.]

1. If anyone causes an abortion in a pregnant woman so that you can immediately recognize whether [the offspring] would have been a boy or a girl: if it was to be a boy, let him compensate with twelve solidi; however, if a girl, [let him compensate] with twenty-four [solidi].

2. If whether [the fetus is male or female] cannot be immediately recognized, and [the fetus] has not changed the shape of the mother's body, let him compensate with twelve solidi. If he seeks more, let him clear himself with oathtakers.

LXXXIX.

[If a woman dies after childbirth, leaving an heir.]

1. If a woman who has a paternal inheritance becomes pregnant after marriage and gives birth to a boy, and she dies in that hour, and the child is alive for a while or for one hour, so that he can open his eyes and see the roof of the house and the four walls, and afterwards dies, let the maternal inheritance remain with the baby's father.

2. Moreover, if his father has witnesses who saw that the child opened his eyes and saw the roof of the house and the four walls, then let the father have permission under the law to hold that property. Whoever the owner is, let him hold his property.

XC.

[If anyone leaves his peer fighting and flees.]

If anyone is engaged in battle while serving in the army, and he leaves his peer fighting and flees, while the latter continues to defend himself, after the latter's return, let him who fled compensate with twice eighty solidi to the other, since he [the latter] did not flee.

XCI.

[If anyone wishes to summon (another) after a case is settled.]

If anyone wishes to summon someone to court after the case is settled and amended [and] after witnesses have testified and compensation is given, if he attempts this and if he cannot defend himself through an oath or through witnesses, then let him defend himself through wager of battle. After this, let the accuser compensate with forty solidi.

XCII.

[If anyone strikes a freewoman with a blow.]

1. If anyone strikes a freewoman with a blow and blood does not flow, let him pay two solidi. Pactus II, 7.
2. If she is a freedwoman, one solidus and a tremissis. Pactus II, 8.
3. If she is a maidservant, let him pay one solidus. Pactus II, 9.
4. If he is a man [*baro*], similarly. Pactus II, 10.
5. If he is a slave, one-half solidus. Pactus II, 11.

XCIII.

[Concerning the stealing of a wheel hub or cart.]

1. If anyone breaks or steals another's wheel hub, let him pay three solidi. Pactus XX, 2.
2. If he steals a cart or breaks the front wheels so that on that day work is hindered, let him compensate with three solidi. Pactus XX, 3.
3. If he steals or breaks the rear [wheels], let him compensate with six solidi. Pactus XX, 4.
4. If it is a harrow, let him compensate with three solidi. Pactus XX, 5.

XCIV.

[If anyone burns or enters a shelter.]

Pactus XXI, 1.

1. If anyone burns a shelter in a forest, whether it is for pigs or cattle, let him compensate with twenty-two solidi.

Pactus XXI, 2, 3.

2. And if he enters with the intention of doing harm and finds nothing of the owner's, let him compensate with six solidi. And if he enters another's courtyard, [let him compensate] in a similar manner.

Pactus XXI, 4, 5.

3. If [he enters] into a storehouse, let him compensate with twelve solidi. If a murderer flees into a courtyard or house, and no one offers a surety for him, and if his pursuer follows him there, he is not to make a claim [against the murderer].

[If anyone offers a herd of pigs or draft horses or cows as a pledge.]

Pactus XXII, 1.

4. If anyone offers a herd of pigs, draft horses, cows, or sheep as a pledge, let him be liable for forty solidi.

Pactus XXII, 2, 3.

5. If a bound swineherd is struck or beaten on the road, and two hold him and a third strikes him, let the swineherd be compensated with nine solidi. And for the rest which he suffers, let him be compensated threefold as [is compensated] for slaves.

Pactus XXII, 4.

6. For herdsmen of sheep, horses, and cows, let them be compensated twice as [is compensated] for slaves.

XCV.

[Concerning the stealing of a bear and other wild animals.]

Pactus XXIII, 1.

1. If anyone steals or kills a bison, a buffalo, [or] a stag that bellows, let him compensate with twelve solidi.

Pactus XXIII, 2.

2. And [if] that stag does not have shackles, let him [the perpetrator] compensate with one-half solidus.

Pactus XXIII, 3.

3. If it has a shackle and is not [killed] by arrows, let him pay one solidus.

Pactus XXIII, 4.

4. If a red deer [is killed] by arrows, let him pay three solidi.

Pactus XXIII, 5.

5. If a black [deer], let him compensate with six solidi.

Pactus XXIII, 6.

6. If it is stolen, let him compensate ninefold.

Pactus XXIV, 1, 2.

7. If a wild doe is killed, let him [the perpetrator] pay a tremissis. If it has a shackle, one-half solidus.

Pactus XXIV, 3.

8. If a red doe [is killed] by arrows, let him pay three solidi.

9. If a black [doe], let him pay six solidi.

Pactus XXIV, 4.

10. If it is stolen, let him compensate ninefold.

Pactus XXIV, 5.

11. If another's bear is killed or stolen, let him pay six solidi. For a wild boar, similarly.

Pactus XXV, 1, 2.

12. If anyone kills a domesticated cow, which is called a lead cow, a boar, or a lead hog, let him compensate with six solidi. If it is stolen, let him pay three solidi; and whatever he [the owner] swears it is worth, let him compensate eightfold [that is, if it is not returned].

Pactus XXV, 3, 4.

13. If anyone kills a roebuck, a saiga. If it is stolen, let him compensate ninefold.

Pactus XXV, 5, 6.

14. If a crane is stolen or killed, let him compensate with three solidi.

Pactus XXVI, 1.

15. If a goose is stolen or killed, let him pay ninefold.

Pactus XXVI, 2.

16. For a duck, jay, stork, raven, crow, dove, and cuckoo, let [compensation] be required as for other similar [birds].

Pactus XXVI, 3.

XCVI.

1. If a hawk kills a goose, let its owner pay three solidi. If [it kills] a crane, let its owner compensate with six solidi.

Pactus XXVI, 4, 5.

2. If a boar kills another boar, let another be returned for it or let three solidi be paid.

Pactus XXVII.

3. If another's dog kills a man, let its owner pay half the wergeld. And if the relatives of the deceased seek the entire wergeld, let all his [the owner of the dog] doors be closed, and let him always enter and leave through one door; and let the dog be hung nine feet above that entrance until it becomes completely putrefied, and drops decayed matter, and its bones lie there. And he cannot enter or leave through any other door. And if he removes the dog from the entrance or enters the house through another door, let him return the other half of the wergeld.

Pactus XXVIII, 1, 2.

[If another's horse kills a man.]

4. If a horse, pig, or ox kills a man, let its owner pay the entire wergeld. If it is a slave [who is killed], let him pay half the slave's price.

Pactus XXIX, 1, 2.

[If (a horse) is pierced jumping over a fence.]

5. If someone's horse jumps over another's fence and is pierced by a stake, let him who owns the fence pay half the price.

Pactus XXX, 1.

Pactus XX, 1.   6. If anyone steals a mill iron, let him replace it along with another and pay six solidi for this theft to him whose it was.

Pactus XXX, 2.   7. If anyone hacks another's fence, let him pay three solidi.

XCVII.

Pactus XXXI, 1.   1. If anyone buries a corpse in foreign ground, let him pay twelve solidi or swear with twelve men that he did not do this with malice.

Pactus XXXI, 2, 3.   2. If anyone sends a freeman or freewoman into another's land without permission from him to whom the land belongs, let him be liable for forty solidi. If he is a slave, let him pay twelve solidi.

Pactus XXXI, 4–6.   3. If anyone [injures] the child of a person from the lower class, let him pay a solidus. If [the child] is from the middle class, let him pay six solidi. If from the highest class, let him pay twelve solidi.

Pactus XXXII, 1, 2.   4. If anyone violently abducts another's girl, let him be liable for her wergeld. If she is not raped [but is still abducted], let him pay twelve[43] solidi.

XCVIII.

Pactus XIX, 1.   1. If anyone intrudes upon another's property or a church in an illegal manner, the man who repels the violence being done commits no crime, since one does no violence defending his own property.

Pactus XIX, 2.   2. Let no one attempt [to intrude upon] another's land without authority; let him who does this know that he is to be expelled with punishment, or [let the owner erect] a boundary.[44]

Here end the Alamannic laws renewed in the time of Lantfrid.

NOTES

Titles

[1] Not all Lantfridana mss. assign the same numbers to the laws. The roman numerals in brackets pertain to the titular numbers given in Codex 8 of the Lantfridana mss. (Lehmann, pp. 37–53), from which I derived the titular descriptions. The roman numerals that accompany bracketed numbers are assigned by Lehmann and have also

been used in this English translation. The roman numerals not accompanied with bracketed numerals, such as I–II, are derived from Codex 8 without modification. The edition of the Alamannic laws given in Eckhardt B is also based on Codex 8 of the Lantfridana mss.

² Codex 8 of the Lantfridana mss. repeats no. LXXIV.

³ Number LXXV is repeated in Codex 8.

Laws

¹ Lantfrid was the duke of the Alamans, 712–30, and the Lantfridana mss. of the Alamannic laws are named after him.

² The Hlotharii mss. give: "Here begin the Alamannic laws, which were promulgated in the time of King Chlotar together with his princes, that is, thirty-three bishops and thirty-four dukes and seventy-two counts and other people." This title from the Hlotharii mss. closely parallels the title of the *Pactus legis Alamannorum* given above.

³ Bestowing property on a church or monastery was a common practice in the Middle Ages. Land or other property so bestowed was confirmed by a charter or letter of confirmation. The written word, therefore, became the legal proof that the new possessor, the church or monastery, was now the legitimate owner. For the Alamans, see the charters in Albert Bruckner and Robert Marichal, eds., *Chartae latinae antiquiores: Facsimile-edition of the Latin Charters prior to the Ninth Century,* part 2, Switzerland: St. Gall-Zurich (Olten and Lausanne, 1956).

⁴ *Fredus* means a fine payable to the government for breaking the peace. It was required in addition to the wergeld.

⁵ The Lantfridana mss. do not present a three-part division of law V. The three-part division furnished in this translation is derived from the *Lex Alamannorum Karolina.* The Lantfridana mss. contain only one short law for law V, which says in its entirety: "If however, any thief forcibly removes within the doors of a church another's property which is entrusted to a church and carries it back to the man to whom it belonged, let him pay just as the law requires. However, let him compensate thirty-six solidi for the injury to the church that suffered the theft." Eckhardt A also renders this short version.

⁶ Only the *Lex Alamannorum Karolina* contains this law. It does not appear in the Lantfridana or Hlotharii mss. It is here numbered V a, although it is law VI in the Karolina tradition. Eckhardt B also numbers it V a. The title contained here is part of the law and is retained in this translation.

⁷ A *denarius* (pl. *denarii*) is a small silver coin, four of which equal a *tremissis.*

⁸ Threefold compensation means that the priest received three times

the payment a freeman would have received for the same crime, since clergy had a higher status than ordinary freemen.

[9] That is, three times the wergeld for the *medianus* Alaman. Since the *medianus* was compensated with a 200-solidi wergeld, the priest received 600 solidi.

[10] Formerly called the response (*responsorium*).

[11] The Marchfield was the place where an assembly of the total armed body of warriors met; it has also been called the Mayfield. It is believed to be a predominantly Frankish institution. Cf. Bernard S. Bachrach, "Was the Marchfield part of the Frankish Constitution?" *Medieval Studies* 36 (1974): 178–85.

[12] A *mancipium* was a slave who worked on a manor. It was from this class of manorial laborers, as well as from the free, although also indentured, *coloni*, that the serf of the Middle Ages emerged. See Robert Boutruche, *Seigneurie et féodalité*, 2d ed., 2 vols (Paris, 1968–1970), 1: 143, n. 27. Cf. Henri Dubled, "*Mancipium* au moyen age," *Revue du moyen age latin* 5 (1949): 51–56.

[13] This title is part of the Lantfridana mss. and is retained in this translation.

[14] *centenarius*. The hundred-man was the military commander in charge of a hundred (*centena*).

[15] Eckhardt B gives forty solidi.

[16] *centena*. The hundred was a judicial district over which the hundred court presided. It was a subdivision of the county. See Theodor Mayer, "Staat und Hundertschaft im fränkischer Zeit," *Rheinische Vierteljahresblätter* 17 (1952): 343–84, reprinted in his *Mittelalterliche Studien: Gesammelte Aufsätze* (Lindau and Constance, 1959), pp. 98–138.

[17] *centenarius*.

[18] *placitum*.

[19] *sabbato in sabbato*.

[20] *septem in septem noctes*.

[21] This title is part of the Lantfridana mss., and it is retained in this translation.

[22] This title is part of the Lantfridana mss.

[23] The Hlotharii mss. have the plural form *solvant* (let them pay) rather than the singular form *solvat* (let him be paid for).

[24] The Hlotharii mss. contain the plural form *conponant* (let them compensate) rather than the singular *solvat* (let him be paid for).

[25] Although the verb is *occiderit* (kills), the law actually describes a particular way of killing—murder. See Lex LXIX below.

[26] The wergeld for women was twice what would be paid for killing men. Since men in these circumstances received ninefold wergeld, women would have received eighteenfold wergeld.

[27] If the husband accepted this payment, the abductor acquired the

guardianship (*mundium*) of the woman. At this point, the crime ceased.

[28] Again, the payment of the 400 solidi gave the abductor legal guardianship over the woman.

[29] It appears that abduction may have been a convenient way to acquire the wife of one's choice without conflict.

[30] Most individuals would not have had possessions equalling 400 solidi. Since payment of even a freeman's wergeld (160 solidi) was usually impossible for one person, the dowry of 400 solidi must have been seen as a maximum, and this for the wealthier classes only.

[31] The Lantfridana mss. spell this as *morginaghepha*. The spelling rendered here is derived from the Hlotharii mss. For the *morgangeba*, see the Glossary.

[32] Eckhardt B gives three solidi.

[33] In all probability, it is the arm below the elbow rather than the elbow which is referred to here. Other mss. render *ante* (before, meaning below) in place of *autem* (however).

[34] This is one of the few instances in the Alamannic laws in which the second person is used. The third person is the predominant form.

[35] Eckhardt A gives eight rather than nine nights.

[36] This title is part of the Lantfridana mss.

[37] The title is part of this law in the Lantfridana mss.

[38] If the child was from the free class, the perpetrator rendered the child's wergeld. If the child was a slave, the perpetrator made restitution with another slave child or paid the wergeld of the dead child.

[39] The clod of earth with the sticks stuck into it is the most obvious symbol in the Alamannic laws. The clod clearly symbolizes land, and the sticks represent vegetation or crops springing from the land.

[40] Other mss. give forty solidi.

[41] Cf. Lex LVII, 68.

[42] Cf. Lex LVII, 40.

[43] Pactus XXXII, 2 from which this law is derived gives forty solidi.

[44] Cf. Pactus XIX, 2. Unlike the Pactus, this law contains the added phrase: *vel habias gadano* (or [let the owner erect] a boundary).

The
Bavarian Laws
as preserved in the
Ingolstadt
Manuscript

In the name of Our Lord Jesus Christ,
here begins the prologue
of the Bavarian laws.

Moses from the tribe of the Hebrews first elucidated the divine laws[1] into sacred writing. King Soron[2] was the first to establish the Greek laws and judgments. Mercurius Trimegistus[3] first gave the Egyptian laws. Solon[4] first gave the Athenian laws. Ligurgus[5] first legislated laws for the Lacedonians in the name of Apollo. Numa Pompilius,[6] who succeeded Romulus[7] in the kingdom, first gave the Roman laws. Since the Roman people could not tolerate the rebellious magistrates, they called together ten men to write the laws, which were translated from Solon's book into the Latin language and were put forth on twelve tables.[8] Moreover, they were these: Appius Claudius, Genutius, Veterius, Julius, Manilius, Sulpitius, Sectius, Curatius, Romelius, and Postumius; these were the ten men chosen to write the law. The laws, however, were arranged in books, first undertaken by the consul Pompeius,[9] but he did not finish because of fear of his rival. Then Caesar[10] began to undertake them, but he was killed before [finishing]. Gradually, however, the Romans repealed the old laws because of their antiquity and neglect, but mentioning them [here] seems necessary, although they are no longer in use. New laws began with Emperor Constantine[11] and the rest of his successors; [yet] they were confusing and without order. Later, Emperor Theodosius the younger[12] promulgated a code of constitutions, modeled upon the Gregorian[13] and Hermogenian[14] codes, from the time of Constantine under a single title for that emperor, which is called by his name: the Theodosian code.[15] Then each people developed their own laws from their customs. An ancient custom, in fact, is to be considered as a law. *Lex* is a written constitution; *mos* is custom derived from antiquity, although an unwritten law. For *lex* is named from *legere,* since it is written. *Mos,* however, means an ancient custom, which is derived only from usage; however, custom is a type of law, defined through usage, from which law is derived. Law should be universal, which alone is established with reason, which serves order, and which produces well-being. Custom is named [i.e., unwritten], but it is in common use.[16] Theoderich,[17] king of the Franks, who was at Châlons,[18] chose wise men within his kingdom who were learned in the ancient law. Under his instruction, he ordered the laws of the Franks, the Alamans, and the Bavarians to be written for each tribe that was under his control, according to his manner; he added what was needed and deleted the unclear and the disorderly. And what pagan customs were there were changed according to Christian law. And what ancient pagan customs King Theoderich did not correct, King Childibert[19] began after this, but King Chlotar[20] completed. All of this Dagobert,[21] the most glorious king, revived through the illustrious men Claudius, Chadoindus, Magnus, and Agilulfus; the best old laws were written down, and he gave each tribe a written law, which still exists today. Laws, moreover, are proclaimed so that boldness may be restrained by human courage, and innocence protected from evil men, and the ability to do harm restrained among evil men by the fear of punishment.[22]

[*Titles*]

   I. Here begin the chapters concerning the books of the established law, which pertain to the clergy or to the rights of churches.

   1. If any free Bavarian wishes to give his freehold or any property to a church, let him have complete authority to do so.

   2. Concerning those who wish to misappropriate a church contrary to law.

3. Concerning thefts of a church: how they are to be compensated.
4. Concerning those who persuade a church slave to flee.
5. Concerning those who kill a church slave who does not deserve capital punishment.
6. Concerning those who burn church property.
7. Concerning those who are [guilty of crime] and take refuge in a church.
8. Concerning the compensation of church servants: how they are to be compensated.
9. Concerning priests, deacons, and also bishops: how they are to be compensated.
10. Concerning bishops only and the killing of them.
11. Concerning nuns or those dedicated to God.
12. Concerning priests and deacons, that they have nothing to do with women.
13. Concerning freemen [*coloni*] and slaves of a church: how they are to serve.

II. Concerning the duke and the cases that pertain to him.

1. If anyone attempts to take the life of the duke.
2. If anyone kills his duke.
3. If anyone stirs up an insurrection.
4. If anyone stirs up a quarrel in the army.
5. If anyone, without the duke's order, plunders the province to which the duke sends the army.
6. If anyone steals something within the army.
7. If anyone dies in the [service][1] of his duke or his lord.
8. If anyone kills a man at the order of the duke.
9. Concerning the duke's sons, if they are impudent.
10. Concerning him who starts a dispute in the duke's courtyard.
11. Let no one raise his hand in wagers of battle without orders.
12. Concerning those who steal something in the duke's courtyard.
13. Concerning those who disregard the duke's order.
14. The court should take place on the first day of the month.
15. That a judge may receive his portion [of a case].
16. How a judge should be appointed.

17. If a judge adjudicates unjustly because of gifts.
18. If he judges wrongly through ignorance.

III.   Concerning families and their compensation.

1. Concerning families, that they receive twofold privilege [of compensation].
2. Concerning the ducal family and their compensation.

IV.   Concerning freemen: how they are to be compensated.

1. If anyone strikes a freeman in anger.
2. If he spills blood.
3. If he lays a hand on him.
4. If he cuts through a vein.
5. If he breaks a bone.
6. If the brain appears.
7. If he binds with rope.
8. If he forcibly holds him.
9. If he knocks out an eye.
10. If he cripples, that is, [if] he cuts off a hand or a foot.[2]
11. Concerning the thumb and the other fingers: how they are to be compensated.
12. Concerning the piercing of the arms.
13. Concerning the nose.
14. Concerning the ear.
15. Concerning the lips.
16. Concerning the teeth.
17. Concerning pushing [another] from a bank.
18. Concerning pulling [someone] off a horse.
19. Concerning pushing [someone] down stairways.
20. Concerning pushing [someone] into fire.
21. Concerning poisoned arrows.
22. Concerning fatal potions.
23. Concerning surrounding [someone] in a hostile manner.
24. Concerning [surrounding someone] in a hostile manner with fewer people.
25. Concerning detaining [people by] force as a pledge.
26. Concerning deceptions, which they call *wancstodal*.
27. Concerning a laming blow.
28. Concerning the killing of freemen.

29. Concerning [the killing] of their women.
30. Concerning foreigners.
31. Concerning the killing of them [foreigners].

    V.   Concerning freedmen who are manumitted: how they are to be compensated.

Nine articles.[3]

    VI.   Concerning slaves: how they are compensated.

Twelve articles.[4]

    VII.   1. Concerning the prohibition of incestuous marriages.[5]
           2. [1.] If he [a man] conducts himself contrary to this [prohibition].[6]
           3. [2.] Concerning lesser persons.[7]
           3a. [I, 14] Concerning Sundays.[8]
           4. [3.] It is not permitted to enslave a freeman who has not committed a felony.[9]

    VIII.   Concerning wives and those cases which often affect them.

1. If anyone lies with another's wife.
2. Concerning slaves who commit this [act].
3. If he lays a hand [on a woman] because of lust.
4. If he lifts her garments above the knees.
5. Concerning [the taking off of] a head covering.
6. Concerning the abduction of a virgin.
7. If anyone abducts a widow.
8. Concerning fornication with freewomen.
9. If a slave fornicates with a freewoman.
10. If he fornicates with a freedwoman.
11. And if with a virgin who is manumitted.
12. If with another's maidservant.
13. If with a virgin maidservant.
14. If he dismisses his own wife.
15. If he does not receive his betrothed.
16. If he abducts another's betrothed.
17. If he deceives [a woman with] a promise.
18. Concerning an abortion by a potion.

19. Various cases of abortion.
20. Concerning wergeld [for abortions].
21. Concerning the prolonged mortification of the relatives.
22. Concerning an abortion by weakness.
23. Concerning an abortion in a maidservant, [let him compensate] as above.

IX.   Concerning theft.

1. If a freeman commits a theft.
2. If he steals from a church.
3. If he steals more valuable property.
4. If he abducts a freeman.
5. If a slave abducts a freeman.
6. A thief taken in the act of theft at night.
7. If he persuades another's slave to steal.
8. If he buys something from a thief unknowingly.
9. If gold or other kinds of property.
10. If he secretly kills another's animal.
11. If he accidentally kills another's animal.
12. Concerning bells.
13. Concerning gardens.
14. Concerning the purchase of stolen property.
15. The same as above.
16. Concerning the custody of stolen property.
17. Concerning compensation from a thief.
18. Oaths are not to be given hastily.
19. Concerning false testimony.
20. Concerning the accusing of another's slave.

X.   Concerning the burning of houses.

1. Concerning setting fire by night.
2. Concerning the storehouses of freemen.
3. Concerning the knocking down of roofs of buildings.
4. Concerning the setting and extinguishing of fires.
5. Concerning the destruction of houses.
6. Concerning roofs.
7. Concerning the posts of roofs.
8. Concerning inside corner posts.
9. Concerning [other posts] of this type.
10. Concerning outside corner [posts].

11. Concerning other [posts] of this type.
12. Concerning beams.
13. Concerning outer [beams], which hold the walls together.
14. Concerning other buildings.
15. Concerning a courtyard.
16. Concerning an outside fence.
17. Concerning a top pole [of a fence].
18. Concerning signs.
19. Concerning a public road.
20. Concerning a side road.
21. Concerning a footpath.
22. Concerning a stream.
23. The same as above.

XI.   Concerning violence.

1. Concerning a courtyard.
2. Concerning a house [if a man enters it by force].
3. As above [a warning against forcible entry].
4. In a similar manner [after the entrant has been judged guilty].

XII.   Concerning the knocking down of boundary markers.

1. Concerning boundary lines.
2. If a slave does this.
3. Concerning a boundary [accidentally leveled].
4. Concerning disputes over boundary markers.
5. Concerning the prohibition of new boundary markers.
6. If a freeman does this.
7. If a slave does this.
8. Concerning unrecognizable markers.
9. Concerning the laying of beams [that is, the hasty construction of a building].
10. Concerning other [buildings] of this kind.
11. Concerning lumber that is not [yet] removed.

XIII.   Concerning pledges.

1. Let no one be allowed to pledge.
2. Concerning one who refuses to render justice.

3. If he accepts a pledge contrary to law.
4. If he accepts pigs as a pledge.
5. If he offers sheep as a pledge.
6. If he plows another's crops or meadow.
7. If he steals a ripe crop.
8. If he performs [magic on] another's crops.
9. If he persuades a slave to flee.

XIV.   Concerning injuries to animals.

1. Concerning injuries to animals.
2. Concerning him who drives it into a fence.
3. If the owner of the fence does this.
4. If it does not die [immediately].
5. If he confesses, let him receive it.
6. Concerning the restoration of animals.
7. If he does not wish to receive the injured animal.
8. If he knocks out an eye from another's animal.
9. If a horn from an ox.
10. If from a cow.
11. If he cuts off a tail [from a horse].
12. Concerning [a horse] of average value.
13. [Concerning a horse] of inferior value.[10]
14. Concerning [the injuring of] a cow in this way.
15. Concerning unjust treatment [of animals].
16. The same as above.
17. Let no one attempt to kill another's animal.

XV.   Concerning commendation.

1. Concerning custody.
2. If he steals gold.
3. [If he steals] from a fire in this way.
4. Concerning the stealing of entrusted property.
5. Concerning regulations [pertaining to a thief within a reasonable period] of time.
6. Concerning property contested in a dispute.
7. Concerning widows.
8. Concerning second marriages.
9. Concerning division among brothers.
10. Concerning him who dies without children.

XVI.   Concerning sales.

1. If one sells another's property.
2. If he sells a possession.
3. If one acquires something from another's slave.
4. Concerning a dispute over acquired property.
5. If one sells a freeman.
6. If [he sells] his own slaves.
7. If a slave buys his freedom with his own property.
8. Concerning an exchange.
9. Concerning the form of a sale.
10. Concerning earnest money.
11. Concerning the affirmation [of sales].
12. The same as above.
13. The same as above.
14. In a similar manner.
15. [A sale] is to be confirmed through a charter or witnesses.
16. Concerning contracts or agreements.
17. Concerning those who sell their own freehold.

XVII.   Concerning witnesses.

1. Concerning witnesses [regarding the entering of another's land].
2. If he wishes to lay his claim.
3. If he has a witness with hearsay evidence.
4. If he is conquered.
5. Where there is disagreement among the judges.
6. If there are more witnesses.

XVIII.   Concerning champions.

1. If one is killed by another.
2. If he is a slave.

XIX.   Concerning dead men and their cases.

1. If anyone digs up a dead man from the grave.
2. If one throws [a dead man] into a river.
3. If he is a slave.
4. Concerning the clothing of the dead.
5. If he injures a corpse [with an arrow].

6. If one injures a corpse [by other means].

7. If he buries a corpse.

8. The same as above.

9. Concerning boats.

10. As above.

XX–XXIII.[11]   Concerning dogs and their compensation. Nine articles. Concerning hawks and other birds. Six articles. Concerning orchards and woods and bees. Eleven articles. Concerning pigs, one article.[12]

This lawbook pertains to the king and his princes and to all the Christian people who live under the Merovingian kingdom.[1]

I.

Here begin the chapters concerning the books of the established law, which pertain to the clergy or to the rights of churches.

[If any free Bavarian wishes to give his freehold or any property to a church, let him have complete authority to do so.]

L. Alam. I, 1.   1. If any free person wishes to give his property to a church for the redemption of his soul, let him have complete control over his own portion as soon as he has accommodated his sons. Let no one prevent him. Neither the king[2] nor anyone else has the right of prohibiting him, and whatever he bestows, that is, estates, land, slaves, or other property, whatsoever he gives for the redemption of his soul, let him confirm this bestowal with his own hand through a charter [letter], and let him call six or more witnesses if he wishes. Let them place their hands on the letter, and let those whom he asks mark their names there. And then let him place this letter on the altar and hand over this property in the presence of the priest who serves there. And hereafter let him have no authority over it, neither him nor his descendants, unless the defender of the church wishes to grant it to him as a benefice; but let the property of a church, whatever is given to a church by Christians, be defended by the bishop.[3]

[Concerning those who wish to misappropriate a church contrary to law.]

2. If any person wishes to misappropriate church property unjustly or to remove church property, whether it is he who gave it or his heirs, or any man attempts this, let him first suffer the judgment of God and the disapproval of the holy Church, and let him pay three ounces of gold to the secular judge and restore this property to the church and add other property equal in value, by order of the king or the prince who is judge in that region.

L. Alam. I, 2.

[Concerning thefts of a church: how they are to be compensated.]

3. If anyone steals church property and he is convicted, let him pay for that property ninefold.[4] And if he wishes to deny it, let him swear as to the worth of the property on the altar of the church from which he stole. Concerning [property with a value of] one saiga, let him swear alone. Concerning two or three saigae and up to one tremissis, let him swear with one oathtaker. Thereafter, up to four tremisses, let him swear with three oathtakers. And if he steals property with a greater value, either a horse, an ox, a cow, or any type of property up to a value of four tremisses, and he wishes to deny it, then let him swear with six oathtakers, and let himself be the seventh, on the altar in the presence of the people and the priest. If, however, he steals something used in the service of the church, that is, a chalice, or paten, or altarcloth, or whatever property he steals from the church, and he is convicted, let him pay thrice ninefold, that is, let him restore three times nine. And if he wishes to deny it, let him swear as to the worth of the property with twelve oathtakers on that altar.

L. Alam. VI.

[Concerning those who persuade a church slave to flee.]

4. If anyone persuades a church slave or maidservant to flee and leads that person beyond the borders, and he is convicted, let him bring the slave back quickly and compensate with fifteen[5] solidi valued in gold, since he attempted to do this. And while he returns that one, let him send another in his place as a pledge until he returns him [the former] whom he induced to flee. And if he cannot find him, then let him give another equal in value and compensate with fifteen[5] solidi. And in the same way concerning a maidservant, let him pay according to her value.

L. Alam. XX.

[*Concerning those who kill a church slave who does not deserve capital punishment.*]

L. Alam. VII.

5. If anyone audaciously kills a church slave who does not deserve capital punishment, let him restore two equal in value for the one he killed. And if he wishes to deny it, let him swear with twelve oathtakers on the altar of the church whose slave he killed.

[*Concerning those who burn church property.*]

6. If anyone, for reasons of hatred, burns church property in a secret manner at night, and it is discovered, if he is a slave, let his hands and his eyes be taken so that he is no longer able to do evil; in fact, let his master restore all property, whatever was burned in that fire. And if a freeman attempts to burn church property, and he is convicted, let him compensate according to this law: let him first give forty solidi valued in gold because of his presumption, since he dared to do such a thing. Then let him compensate for every roof that falls in that fire with twenty-four solidi; and let him restore all things that were burned there with equal value. And let him compensate each man who was within there and escaped uninjured from the fire with his *hrevavunti*. And if anyone is injured or killed there, let him compensate according to the class of each, if it is done with his own hand. And if he wishes to deny this, let him swear with twenty-four designated oathtakers on the altar with the New Testament in the presence of the defender of the church. And whoever is convicted of theft of church property, let him offer security for a portion of the *fredus* to the public treasury, and let him give a pledge worth forty solidi, and let him pay as much as the judge orders. And the more strictly he pays, the firmer will be the peace of the church.

[*Concerning those who are (guilty of crime) and take refuge in a church.*]

L. Alam. III,
1–3.

7. If anyone guilty of crime takes refuge in a church, let no one dare to remove him through force after he enters the door of a church, until one queries a priest of the church or a bishop. If a priest takes the responsibility of replying, and if [the fugitive] is guilty and worthy of punishment, let one follow this [course of action] with the consent of the priesthood, since he took refuge in a church. Let no crime be so grave that life is not granted him

because of fear of God and reverence of the saints, since the Lord says: "Whoever forgives, it will be forgiven him; whoever does not forgive, it will not be forgiven him."[6] If, however, any stubborn and proud man has no fear [of God] or reverence for a holy church, and removes his fleeing slave or whomever he pursues from a church with force, and does not give honor to God, let him compensate with forty solidi to that church at the order of a judge and forty solidi to the public treasury as a *fredus*, so that there may be honor to God and reverence of the saints, and so that God's Church may always be invincible.

[*Concerning the compensation of church servants: how they are to be compensated.*]

8. If anyone harms, strikes, injures, or kills servants of a church, that is, a subdeacon, lector, exorcist, acolyte, doorkeeper, or any of these, let him compensate twice what their relatives are customarily compensated. Those who are servants of God's altar, let them receive double compensation; let the other clergy, however, be compensated just as their relatives are. Monks, however, who live according to a rule in a monastery are compensated twofold according to their family, so that reverence may be given to God and peace maintained by those who serve Him.

L. Alam. XIV, XV, 1, 2.

[*Concerning priests, deacons, and also bishops: how they are to be compensated.*]

9. If anyone harms or injures a priest or a deacon whom a bishop appoints in a parish or whom the people take to themselves as a priest and whom the ecclesiastical see approved, let him compensate for him threefold. If he kills him, let him pay for a priest 300 solidi valued in gold; if he has no gold, let him give other property, slaves, land, or whatever he has, until he fulfills it. For deacons, however, let him pay 200 solidi both to that church where they were servants at the requirement of the bishop appointed in that province, and to the duke. And for a *fredus*, let him pay fifty[7] solidi to the state, so that thereafter reverence for priests and honor to a church may not be disregarded, and no presumption may grow among the people.

L. Alam. XII, XIII.

[*Concerning bishops only and the killing of them.*]

10. If anyone kills a bishop whom the king appointed or the people chose to be a high priest, let him pay for him to the king,

L. Alam. XI.

the people, or his relatives according to this decree. Let a leaden garment be made according to his status, and let him give as much as it weighs in gold for the man whom he killed; and if he does not have gold, let him give other property, slaves, land, villas, or whatever he has, until he fulfills the debt. And if he does not have that much property, let him place himself in slavery to that church, with his wife and his sons, until he can redeem them. Let this be done through an order of the king or a judge, and let the property be permanently affixed for the use of the church where he was high priest. And if a bishop appears guilty before another, let him [the latter] not attempt to kill him, since he is the highest priest, but let him summon the bishop before the king or the duke or before his people. And if he, being convicted of a crime, cannot deny it, then let him be judged according to church law. If he is guilty of such a crime, let him be deposed or exiled. Concerning homicide, fornication, high treason, or inviting enemies into the province, so that he wishes to lose those whom he should save, let him be punished for these crimes.

[*Concerning nuns or those dedicated to God.*]

11.[8] If anyone abducts a nun from a convent, that is, one dedicated to God, and takes her as a wife for himself against ecclesiastical law, let the bishop of that diocese with the consent of the king or the duke demand her back. Nevertheless, let him give her back to the convent from which he abducted her, whether he wants to or not, and let him compensate twofold to that convent what is customarily compensated by one who steals another's betrothed. We know that the abduction of another's betrothed is a punishable crime; how much more punishable is a crime which usurps the betrothed of Christ. And if he does not wish to compensate and return her, let him be expelled from the province, [since] the apostle says: "Put away evil from yourselves,"[9] and another time: "Deliver such a man to Satan for the destruction of the flesh, so that the spirit may be saved in the day of our Lord Jesus Christ."[10]

[*Concerning priests and deacons, that they have nothing to do with women.*]

12.[11] Concerning priests, deacons, and ecclesiastical servants. Let no priest or deacon be allowed to have a strange [non-familial] woman with him in his house; neither let him be led through that opportunity and offer polluted sacrifice, nor let the people sink through his offense and suffer harm. For this reason, concerning those who are invested with priestly rank, let them know that cohabitation with strange women is forbidden. Only this permission is allowed them: that they may lodge within the walls of their houses mothers, daughters, and full sisters. Concerning these, in fact, no unfortunate offenses are feared, since agreement with nature is allowed. Love does not jeopardize their chastity. In other cases concerning priests, deacons, or clergy, let them be judged by a bishop according to ecclesiastical law.

[*Concerning freemen* (coloni) *and slaves of a church: how they are to serve.*]

13. Concerning freemen [*coloni*] or slaves of a church: how L. Alam. XXI. they are to serve or how they render tribute.[12] There is the grain tax rendered according to the estimate of the judge. Let the judge provide this: according to what one has, let him give. For thirty pecks let him give three, and let him pay the pasture tax according to the custom of the province. For a lawful acre, that is, computed on a ten-foot rod, four rods in width, forty in length, let him plow, sow, enclose, harvest, draw in, and store away.[13] Each tenant is obligated for two pecks of grain from planting up to a tremissis [land worth one tremissis] and to sow and harvest it, and to plant, dig up, graft and prune vines, and to gather in the vintage. Let them render a bundle of linen, ten jars of honey, four chickens, and fifteen eggs. Let them give horses, or let them go where they are ordered to go. Let them render compulsory service with horse-drawn wagons up to fifty miles; let them not be required to go further. Let them undertake a reasonable [amount of work] repairing the lord's buildings, that is, hayloft, granary, or enclosure, and when it is necessary, let them rebuild all these structures. For a lime oven, if it is near, let fifty men bring firewood or stone. Where the distance is greater, let a hundred men carry it, and let them carry lime to a district or estate where it is needed. However, let slaves of a church render tribute according to their possessions. Let them work three days a week on the demesne, three days for themselves. If, however, their lord gives them oxen or other property which he has, let them serve only within the limits of possibility. Nevertheless, let no one be oppressed unjustly.

II.

Concerning the duke and the cases that pertain to him.

[*If anyone attempts to take the life of the duke.*]

L. Alam. XXIII.   1. If anyone attempts to take the life of the duke whom the king appoints to that province or whom the people themselves choose as duke, and he is convicted so that he cannot deny it, let that man and his life be in the power of the duke, and let his property be confiscated by the state. And this is not to occur as an incidental provocation, but let the proven fact reveal the truth. And let it not be proven with one witness, but with three witnesses, all of equal class. If, however, one witness testifies and another denies it, then let them resort to the judgment of God, and let them go to the field, and let God give victory to whomever is to be believed. And let this take place in the presence of the people, so no one may die through malice. Let no free Bavarian lose his freehold land or his life [unless punishable for] a capital offense; that is, attempting to take the life of the duke, inviting enemies into the province, or devising to seize the state through foreign intervention. And [if] he is convicted, then let his life be in the power of the duke, and let all his property [descend] into the treasury. Moreover, for other offenses that he commits, let him compensate according to the law, as long as he has property. If, however, he has no property, let him be pressed into slavery, and let him serve that one whom he injured several months and years, if he was able to profit [from his act], until he restores the whole debt.

[*If anyone kills his duke.*]

2. If anyone kills his duke, let his life be taken for the homicide he caused, and let his property be permanently confiscated by the state.

[*If anyone stirs up an insurrection.*]

3. If anyone stirs up an insurrection against his duke, which the Bavarians call *carmulum,* let him by whom it is first provoked compensate 600 solidi to the duke. Concerning all other men of the same class who followed and kept counsel with him, let each compensate with 200 solidi. Let lesser persons who followed him

and are free compensate with forty solidi, so that a rebellion may not arise in the province.

[*If anyone stirs up a quarrel in the army.*]

4. If anyone in the army that the king or duke appoints in the province stirs up a quarrel within his own band, and men are killed there, let him compensate with 600 solidi to the state. And whoever causes beatings or injuries or commits homicide there, let him compensate each according to his class, just as the law requires. And let a man who does this extol the king or his duke as merciful if he grants him his life. Concerning lesser men, however, if they stir up a quarrel in the army, let it be in the power of the duke [to decide] which punishment they are to endure. For this practice must be eradicated, so that it does not occur. A quarrel frequently arises, in fact, over horse fodder or firewood, since some [soldiers] are assigned to defend farm buildings and barns, where hay and grain are found. This [disagreement] is forbidden so that a quarrel does not occur. If anyone finds fodder or firewood, let him take what he wishes, and let no one be prevented from taking [what he wants], so that a quarrel may not occur because of this. If anyone dares to do this and opposes this in some way that the law forbids, then let him, if he is discovered, be liable to military law in the presence of the duke or before his court; that is, let him receive fifty lashes.[14]

L. Alam. XXV, 1.

[*If anyone, without the duke's order, plunders the province to which the duke sends the army.*]

5. If anyone in the army wishes through hostility to plunder the province without his duke's order, or to take hay or grain or burn buildings, we forbid this totally, and it is not to occur. And hereafter let a count be careful [of its happening] in his retinue;[15] in fact, let him give his order to a hundred-man[16] and a ten-man,[17] and let each one watch over the troops that he commands so they do not act contrary to law. And if anyone does this audaciously, it [the act] is to be examined by the count whose man does it. And if the count neglects to inquire[18] who does this, let him restore all things from his own property; nevertheless, let him have time to investigate. And if such a powerful man does this that a count cannot restrain him, then let him tell his duke, and let the duke restrain him according to law. If he is a freeman, let him owe

forty solidi, and let him restore all things with equal value. If a slave does this, let him be sentenced to capital punishment. Let his master, however, restore all things equally, since he did not forbid his slave to do such things. If you devour one another, you will perish quickly.[19] Nevertheless, let a count not neglect to watch over his army, so that it does not act contrary to law within his province.

[*If anyone steals something within the army.*]

L. Alam. XXVI, 1.

6. If anyone steals something [within][20] the army, either a hobble, halter, bridle, blanket, or whatever, and he is convicted, if he is a slave, let him lose his hands; however, let his master return that property if he has it. If, however, a freeman does this, let him redeem his hands with forty solidi, and let him return what he stole.

[*If anyone dies in the (service)[21] of his duke or his lord.*]

7. If a man is sent forth in the army in the service of his lord, wherever his lord sends him, and he dies there, and he sought to do the honor of his lord or his people, his heirs are never to be cut off from his inheritance, whatever their class is, but let the duke defend them until they can themselves. Then, in fact, let no one hesitate to do the will of his lord because he hopes to receive a gift if he escapes alive. And if he dies, let him be assured that his sons and daughters will possess his inheritance without difficulty; then let him fulfill the order faithfully and promptly.

[*If anyone kills a man at the order of the duke.*]

8. If anyone kills a man at the order of the king or the duke who has that province in his power, let him not be questioned in an investigation or be involved in a feud, since it was at the order of his duke and he cannot disobey the order; rather, let the duke defend him and his sons. And if that duke dies, let the other duke who follows in his place defend him.

[*Concerning the duke's sons, if they are impudent.*]

L. Alam. XXXV, 1, 2.

9. If a duke's son is so proud or foolish, that he wishes to remove his father through evil-minded intention or force and wishes to take his dukedom away from him, while his father is still able

to contest in a judgment, lead the army, judge the people, mount a horse manfully, and command his weapons vigorously, is not deaf nor blind, and can execute the king's orders in every way: let that son know that he acted contrary to law and that he is excluded from his father's inheritance, and nothing of his father's property belongs to him any longer. And let it be within the power of his father to exile him if he wishes. Let him have nothing in his power except what his father wishes to give him through pity. And if he survives his father and has other brothers, let them not give him a portion, since he sinned against his father contrary to law. And if that man, being the only heir, survives his father, let it be in the power of the king to give [the inheritance] to whomever he wishes, either to that man or to another.

[*Concerning him who starts a dispute in the duke's courtyard.*]

10. If anyone through arrogance or drunkenness starts a dispute in the duke's courtyard, so that a fight arises there, let him compensate for whatever occurs there according to the law, and let him compensate forty solidi to the state because of his folly. If it is someone's slave who starts this, let him lose his hand. Let no one attempt to start a dispute in the duke's courtyard.

L. Alam. XXXIII.

[*Let no one raise his hand in wagers of battle without orders.*]

11. If anyone in the duke's courtyard, or wherever they fight wagers of battle [juridical duels], raises his hand before he who is supervising [the duel] orders it, if he is a freeman, let him compensate forty solidi to the state; if he is a slave, let him lose his right hand, or let his lord redeem him with forty[22] solidi. Such action from which a dispute can arise is forbidden.

[*Concerning those who steal something in the duke's courtyard.*]

12. If anyone steals something within the duke's courtyard, since the duke's house is a public building, let him compensate thrice ninefold, that is, let a freeman compensate three times nine. However, if he is a slave, let him pay ninefold, or let him lose his hand. And if he finds something in the duke's courtyard apparently cast aside through neglect, and he carries it off and conceals it by night, let it be regarded as a theft; let him compensate fifteen solidi to the state.

L. Alam. XXX, XXXI.

[Concerning those who disregard the duke's order.]

L. Alam. XXVII, 1.

13. If anyone disregards an order of his duke, his sign, which is used to transmit the duke's orders, his ring, or his seal, and he refuses to come or to do what is ordered of him, let him give fifteen solidi for his negligence to the state, and then let him carry out the order.

[The court should take place on the first day of the month.]

L. Alam. XXXVI, 1, 3.

14. The court should take place on the first day of the month or after fifteen days, if it is necessary for investigating disputes, so that there may be peace in the province. And let all freeman assemble where the judge orders on the established day; and let no one who lives within the county (whether vassals of the king or the duke) neglect to come to court. All should come to court. And whoever neglects to come, let him be fined fifteen solidi. Let a count have a judge with him who is appointed to judge there, and [let him bring] the lawbook, so that he may always render judgment correctly. Whoever opposes the law, let him compensate all disputes as the law requires, and let him give a pledge to that count for the *fredus* the law requires.

[That a judge may receive his portion (of a case).]

15. Moreover, let a judge receive his portion from a case which he judges. From three solidi, let him receive one tremissis; from six solidi, let him receive two tremisses; from nine solidi, let him receive one solidus. From all compensations let him always receive a ninth part, so long as he judges correctly.

[How a judge should be appointed.]

L. Alam. XLI, 1.

16. Moreover, let such a man be appointed judge who judges truth according to this edict: let him not be bribed or greedy. The law perishes from a love of gain; favors and gifts take away the force of the laws; unjust living remains unpunished. For this reason, let such a man be appointed judge who values justice more than money.

[If a judge adjudicates unjustly because of gifts.]

L. Alam. XLI, 1.

17. If a judge adjudicates wrongly after accepting a bribe, let that man who took something unjustly from another through

juridical decision restore what he obtained. Let a judge who ad-judicates falsely be compelled to pay twofold to him who suffered a loss, since he attempted to pass judgment against the regulations of our law. And let him be compelled to pay forty solidi into the public treasury.

[*If he judges wrongly through ignorance.*]

18. If, however, he judges unjustly, neither through favor nor cupidity but through error, let the judgment in which he is known to have erred have no effect; let the judge be free from blame.

III.

Concerning families and their compensation.

[*Concerning families, that they receive twofold privilege (of compensation).*]

1. Concerning families and their compensation. Concerning the families who are called Hosi, Draozza, Fagana, Hahilinga, Anniona. These are, so to speak, the first after the Agilolfinga,[23] who are of the ducal family; to these, in fact, we grant a double honor, and, therefore, they receive double compensation. How-ever, let one compensate the Agilolfingi up to the duke fourfold, since they are the highest princes among you. The duke, more-over, who is first among the people, is and always ought to be from the family of the Agilolfingi, as it was granted to their family by the kings, our ancestors, that the duke rule over the people;[24] they are faithful and suitable to the family of the king. And because of this, since he is duke, let greater honor be given to his immediate family than to his other relatives, so that a third part is to be added to the compensation for his relatives given above. If the lives of his relatives are taken, let them be compen-sated with 640[25] solidi.

[*Concerning the ducal family and their compensation.*]

2. The duke, however, is to be compensated to his relatives with 900[26] solidi or, if he has no relatives, to the king, and ac-cording to this edict other compensations are to follow, just as his relatives are customarily compensated. Thus, if a case occurs con-cerning the duke and one equal in rank, let him compensate them

thus: where the compensation of his relatives is four solidi, the duke's is consequently six; where theirs is six solidi, the duke's is consequently nine; where theirs is as much as twelve solidi,[27] the duke's, consequently, is eighteen. Thus let a third part [*i.e.,* half again as much] always be added in cases of the duke, even to the most extreme litigation which customarily occurs among men.

IV.

Concerning freemen: how they are to be compensated.

[*If anyone strikes a freeman in anger.*]

L. Alam. LVII, 1.

1. If anyone strikes a freeman in anger, which they call *pulislac,* let him give one solidus.

[*If he spills blood.*]

L. Alam. LVII, 2.

2. If he spills his blood, which they call *plotruns,* let him compensate with one and one-half solidi.

[*If he lays a hand on him.*]

L. Alam. LVIII.

3. If he lays a hand on him contrary to law, which they call *infanc,* let him give three solidi.

[*If he cuts through a vein.*]

L. Alam. LVII, 3, 34, 35.

4. If he cuts through his vein so that he cannot stop [the blood][28] without a cauterizing iron, which they call *adarcrati;*[29] if the skull appears on the head, which they call *kepolsceni;* if he breaks a bone and the skin is not broken, which they call *palcprust;* and if he causes such an injury that a swelling results: if any of these things happen, let him compensate with six solidi.

[*If he breaks a bone.*]

L. Alam. LVII, 4.

5. If he breaks a bone of the head or upper arm with a blow, let him compensate with six solidi.

[*If the brain appears.*]

L. Alam. LVII, 6, 55.

6. If the brain of the head appears or the internal organs are injured, which they call *hrevavunt,* let him compensate with twelve solidi.

[*If he binds with rope.*]

7. If anyone binds him with rope contrary to law, let him compensate with twelve solidi.

[*If he forcibly holds him.*]

8. If he forcibly holds him [and he (the former) does not bind him],[30] which they call *hraopant,* let him compensate with six solidi.

[*If he knocks out an eye.*]

9. If anyone knocks out an eye of a freeman or cuts off a hand or a foot, let him compensate with forty solidi.

L. Alam. LVII, 14, 66.

[*If he cripples, that is, (if) he cuts off a hand or a foot.*]

10. And if it is such an injury or such a break that he is crippled thereafter, let him compensate with twenty solidi.

L. Alam. LVII, 38.

[*Concerning the thumb and the other fingers: how they are to be compensated.*]

11. If anyone cuts off someone's thumb, let him compensate with twelve solidi. And if he cuts off a forefinger or a little finger, let him compensate with nine solidi, the one [finger] as well as the other. [Let him compensate][31] for the two middle fingers with ten solidi, the one with five [solidi][32] and the other with five. And if they are cut off and [one finger] is crippled, that is, stands rigid, so that he cannot bend it, and this becomes a hindrance to bearing arms, compensation is greater than for abscission; let a third part be added to the above. To twelve solidi add four, making sixteen; to nine add three, making twelve; to five add two solidi and one tremissis, making seven [solidi][33] and one tremissis: thus one ought to judge and to compensate.

L. Alam. LVII, 42, 45, 48, 51–53.

[*Concerning the piercing of the arms.*]

12. If anyone pierces another's arm above the elbow, let him compensate with six solidi. If he pierces below the elbow, let him compensate with three solidi.

L. Alam. LVII, 31, 32.

[*Concerning the nose.*]

L. Alam. LVII, 15.

13. If anyone pierces someone's nose, let him compensate with nine solidi.

[*Concerning the ear.*]

L. Alam. LVII, 8, 10.

14. If anyone pierces the ear, let him compensate with three solidi. If he cuts off someone's ear, let him compensate with twenty solidi. If he injures him so that he becomes deaf thereafter, let him compensate with forty solidi. If he mutilates the ear so that it appears disfigured, which they call *lidiscart*,[34] let him compensate with six solidi.

[*Concerning the lips.*]

L. Alam. LVII, 11, 12, 18, 19, 26.

15. A lower lip is to be compensated in the same way, and a lower eyelid in a similar manner.[35] If he injures it so that it cannot hold tears or a lower lip [so that it] cannot hold saliva, then let him compensate with six solidi. If he, however, disfigures an upper eyelid or upper lip, let him compensate with three solidi.

[*Concerning the teeth.*]

L. Alam. LVII, 22, 23, 59.

16. If anyone knocks out someone's maxillary tooth, which they call *marchzand,* let him compensate with twelve solidi. However, [if][36] he knocks out other teeth, let him compensate with six solidi for each one.[37]

[*Concerning pushing (another) from a bank.*]

17. If anyone pushes another from a bank or from a bridge into water, which the Bavarians call *inunwan,* let him compensate with twelve solidi.

[*Concerning pulling (someone) off a horse.*]

L. Alam. LIX, 1.

18. If anyone pulls someone from his horse, which they call *marchfalli,*[38] let him compensate with six solidi.

[*Concerning pushing (someone) down stairways.*]

19. And if he unjustly throws someone down a stairway or any kind of ascent, and that man is thrown from above, which they call *inunwan,* let him compensate with twelve solidi.

[*Concerning pushing (someone) into fire.*]

20. Likewise, if he pushes someone into fire, so that the flames leap above his head, let him compensate with twelve solidi.

[*Concerning poisoned arrows.*]

21. If anyone sheds someone's blood with poisoned arrows, let him compensate with twelve solidi, since for this reason it is *inunwan.*[39]

[*Concerning fatal potions.*]

22. Likewise, whoever gives someone a potion of the type in which is to be found a fatal poison, whether it is a small or large amount, if he [the latter] escapes with his life, let [the poisoner] compensate with twelve solidi.

[*Concerning surrounding (someone) in a hostile manner.*]

23. If anyone surrounds a freeman with a hostile band, which they call *heriraita,* that is, one with forty-two men [literally, shields], and shoots an arrow or any type of missile whatsoever into a courtyard, let him compensate with forty solidi; moreover, let him pay just as much to the duke.

[*Concerning (surrounding someone) in a hostile manner with fewer people.*]

24. If, however, there are fewer men [literally, shields], by whom he is unjustly and forcibly surrounded, which they call *heimzuht,* let him be compensated with twelve solidi.

[*Concerning detaining (people by) force as a pledge.*]

25. If anyone holds a freeman contrary to law by force as a pledge, or detains him in a house or similar place so that he does not have free departure, let him compensate with forty solidi.

[*Concerning deceptions, which they call* wancstodal.]

26. If any freeman flees from the presence of his enemies, and another urges him to resist by force or deceives him, and in the meantime his [the former's] enemies gather together and kill him,

and the other has done nothing more or involved himself in [the incident], and he has not defended him, which they call *wancstodal,* let him compensate with twelve solidi to his relatives.

[*Concerning a laming blow.*]

L. Alam. LVII, 62.

27. If anyone injures someone so that he becomes lame thereafter and his foot drags on the ground [literally, through the dew], which they call *taudregil,*[40] let him compensate with twelve solidi.

[*Concerning the killing of freemen.*]

L. Alam. LX, 1.

28. If anyone kills a freeman, let him pay his [the victim's] relatives, if he has any; if, however, he does not have any, let him pay the duke or the man to whom he was commended,[41] twice eighty solidi, which is 160.

[*Concerning (the killing) of their women.*]

L. Alam. LX, 2.

29. If any of these acts happens to the women of those freemen, let all be compensated for twofold. Since a woman cannot defend herself with weapons, let her obtain a double compensation. If, however, she wishes to fight through boldness of heart, just as a man does, her compensation will not be twofold.

[*Concerning foreigners.*]

30. Concerning foreigners passing on a road. In fact, let no one dare to annoy or harm a foreigner; some pass by on a journey of religious nature, others because of need, yet safe passage ought to be accorded to all. If, however, someone threatens to harm a foreigner and does—either robs, injures, wounds, confines, sells, or kills him—and he is convicted, let him be compelled to pay 160 solidi to the public treasury; and if he abandons a foreigner still living, let him compensate twofold to him for all the injustice which he did him or for what he stole, just as he [the foreigner] is customarily compensated outside the province.

[*Concerning the killing of them (foreigners).*]

31. If, however, he kills him, let him be compelled to pay one hundred solidi valued in gold. If relatives are lacking, let him pay the public treasury, and on account of this crime let him distribute property to the poor so that he can have the Lord's favor, who

said: "You shall not mistreat a foreigner and stranger."[42] If the duke permits him to keep anything, let him compensate with eighty solidi from his property.

V.

Concerning freedmen who are manumitted: which they call frilaz.[43]

1. If anyone strikes him [a freedman], which they call *pulislac,* let him compensate with one-half solidus.

L. Alam. LVII, 1.

2. If he, in fact, spills blood, let him compensate with eight and one-half saigae.

L. Alam. LVII, 2.

3. If he lays a hand on him contrary to law, which they call *infanc,* or if he injures him so that because of this he seeks a physician, or so that the skull appears on the head, or a vein is cut through, let him compensate with one and one-half solidi.

L. Alam. LVII, 3; LVIII.

4. If he deals him such a wound that, because of it, a bone of the head or one from the upper arm becomes broken, let him compensate with three solidi.

L. Alam. LVII, 4.

5. If anyone strikes him so that his brain appears, or injures the internal organs, which they call *hrevavunt,* or binds him contrary to law, let him compensate with six solidi.

L. Alam. LVII, 6, 55.

6. If anyone knocks out his eye or cuts off a hand or foot, let him compensate with ten solidi.

L. Alam. LVII, 14, 66.

7. If anyone cuts off someone's thumb, let him compensate with six solidi. For a forefinger and little finger, let him compensate with one and one-half[44] solidi. For the two middle fingers, let him compensate with one solidus.

L. Alam. LVII, 42, 45, 48, 51, 52.

8. If anyone injures [him],[45] so that he remains lame thereafter and his foot drags on the ground [literally, through the dew], let him compensate with six solidi.

L. Alam. LVII, 62.

9. If he kills him, let him compensate for him to his lord with forty solidi.[46]

L. Alam. LX, 1.

VI.

Concerning slaves: how they are to be compensated.[47]

1. If anyone strikes another's slave in anger, let him compensate with one tremissis.

L. Alam. LVII, 1.

L. Alam. LVII, 2.

2. If he spills blood, let him give one-half solidus.

L. Alam. LVII, 3; LVIII.

3. If he commits *infanc* towards him contrary to law, or wounds him on the head so that the skull appears, or cuts through a vein, or causes a swollen wound, let him compensate with one solidus.

L. Alam. LVII, 4.

4. If he deals him such a wound that thereafter he causes a fractured bone, let him compensate with one and one-half solidi.

L. Alam. LVII, 6, 55.

5. If he injures him so that the brain appears, or he injures the internal organs, which they call *hrevavunt,* and if he strikes and beats him so much that he leaves him half dead, let him compensate for this with four[48] solidi.

L. Alam. LVII, 14, 66.

6. If he knocks out his eye or cuts off a hand or foot, let him compensate with six[49] solidi.

L. Alam. LVII, 45, 48, 51, 52.

7. [6.] [50]For a forefinger and little finger, let him compensate with two solidi, and for the two middle fingers, let him compensate with one and one-half[51] solidi.

L. Alam. LVII, 15.

8. [7.] If he pierces his nose, let him compensate with two[52] solidi.

L. Alam. LVII, 10–12, 18, 19.

9. If he disfigures a lower lip, an ear, or lower eyelid, let him compensate with one and one-half solidi; however, for the upper [lip or eyelid], let him compensate with one solidus.

L. Alam. LVII, 22, 23.

10. If he knocks out his maxillary tooth, which they call *marchzand,* let him compensate with three solidi. However, for the others, let him compensate with one and one-half solidi.

L. Alam. LVII, 8, 9, 62.

11. If he cuts off his ear, let him compensate with one and one-half solidi. If he pierces his ear, let him compensate with one solidus. If he deafens him or injures him so that he remains lame, which they call *taudregil,*[53] and if he pushes him from a bank or bridge into water, let him always compensate in these cases with four solidi.

L. Alam. LX, 1.

12. If he kills him, let him pay for him with twenty solidi to his lord.[54]

VII.

Concerning the prohibition of illicit marriages
[and work on Sunday].[55]

[Concerning the prohibition of incestuous marriages.]

L. Alam. XXXIX.

1.[56] We prohibit incestuous marriages. Accordingly, it is not permitted to have as wife a mother-in-law, daughter-in-law, step-daughter, step-mother, brother's daughter, sister's daughter, brother's wife, or wife's sister. Brother's children and sister's children are under no pretext to be joined together.

[*If he (a man) conducts himself contrary to this (prohibition).*]

2. If anyone acts against this, let them [the married pair] be separated by the judges in that place, and let them lose all their property, which the public treasury shall acquire.

L. Alam. XXXIX.

[*Concerning lesser persons.*]

3. If there are lesser persons who pollute themselves through an illicit union, let them lose their freedom; let them be added to the public slaves.

L. Alam. XXXIX.

[*Concerning Sundays.*]

3a. [I, 14.] If anyone does servile work on Sunday for a freeman, if he yokes oxen and drives about in a cart, let him lose the right-hand ox. If, however, he cuts or collects hay, or cuts and collects a harvest, or does any servile work on Sunday, let him be warned once or twice. And if he does not correct himself, let him be beaten upon his back with fifty blows, and if he presumes to work on Sunday again, let a third of his property be carried off. And if he still does not cease, then let him lose his freedom and be a slave, because he does not wish to be free on a holy day. If he is a slave, however, let him be flogged for such a crime. And if he does not correct himself, let him lose his right hand, since such acts are prohibited that incite God to anger, and, furthermore, we will be punished regarding our crops and afflicted with want. Thus, this [work] is forbidden on Sunday. And if one is taking a journey with a cart or boat, let him pause from Sunday until Monday. And if he does not wish to observe the Lord's command, because the Lord has said, "No work shall you do on the holy day, neither you nor your servant nor your maidservant nor your ox nor your ass nor any which is subject to you,"[57] and if he neglects to observe this either on a journey or anywhere, let him be fined twelve solidi. And if he does this frequently, let him be fined the punishment described above.

L. Alam. XXXVIII.

[It is not permitted to enslave a freeman who has not committed a felony.]

4. Let it not be permitted to enslave a freeman who has not committed a felony, nor to disperse his inheritance; rather, freemen who observe just laws shall possess their inheritance without hindrance. Although he is poor, let him not lose his freedom or his inheritance, unless he wishes to hand it over to someone voluntarily; let him have the authority to do this. Whoever acts contrary to this command, let either the duke, the judge, or any person know that he has acted contrary to law. Let him owe forty[58] solidi to the state; and let him restore the freeman, whom he oppressed with slavery and from whose property he took away, to his former liberty, and let him restore with equal value the property he took unjustly; let him compensate with forty solidi [the man] he enslaved contrary to law.

VIII.

Concerning wives and those cases which often affect them.

[If anyone lies with another's wife.]

1. If anyone lies with another's freewoman, if it is discovered, let him compensate with the wergeld of that wife to the husband. And if he is killed in bed with her, let him lie in his crime without further punishment or compensation to her husband. And if he places one foot on the bed and is prevented by the woman and does nothing more, let him compensate with fifteen[59] solidi, since he trod unjustly on another's marriage bed.

[Concerning slaves who commit this (act).]

2. If a slave does this and is killed with a freewoman in another's marriage bed, let the wergeld of that wife be diminished by twenty solidi for her damages; however, let his master be compelled to pay what remains until the amount of the compensation is paid. And if that slave escapes and is not killed, but nevertheless is convicted of the crime, let his master nevertheless return him to the man whose wife he disgraced in place of the twenty solidi. However, let him [the master] fulfill all conditions, since he did not impose discipline on his slave.

[If he lays a hand (on a woman) because of lust.]

3. If anyone lays a hand on a freewoman because of lust, or on   L. Alam. LVI, 1.
a virgin or another's wife, which the Bavarians call *horcrif*,[60] let
him compensate with six solidi.

[If he lifts her garments above the knees.]

4. If he lifts her garments above the knees, which they call   L. Alam. LVI, 1.
himilzorunga,[61] let him compensate with twelve solidi.

[Concerning (the taking off of) a head covering.]

5. If, however, he takes off a head covering from her head,   L. Alam. LVI, 1.
which they call *walcuurf*,[62] or lustfully seizes a virgin's hair, let
him compensate with twelve solidi.

[Concerning the abduction of a virgin.]

6. If anyone abducts a virgin against her or her relatives' will,   L. Alam. LIII, 1.
let him compensate with forty solidi, and let him be compelled to
pay another forty solidi into the public treasury.

[If anyone abducts a widow.]

7. If, however, one abducts a widow who is compelled to leave
her house because of her children and her poverty, let him compensate with eighty solidi, and let him be compelled to pay forty
solidi to the public treasury, since such recourse is forbidden and
[her] protection must depend on God, the duke, and the judges.

[Concerning fornication with freewomen.]

8. If anyone fornicates with a freewoman with her consent and   L. Alam. LVI, 1.
does not wish to take her in marriage, let him compensate with
twelve solidi, since he is not yet betrothed nor married by his
parents, but is defiled in his lust.

[If a slave fornicates with a freewoman.]

9. If a slave fornicates with a freewoman, and this fact is discovered, let the slave's owner return the slave to her relatives for
the punishment he deserves or to be killed. And let the owner be
compelled to pay nothing more, since such crimes excite hostility
among the people.

[If he fornicates with a freedwoman.]

10. If he lies with a freedwoman, whom they call *frilaza,* and she has a husband, let him compensate with forty solidi to her relatives[63] or to her husband.

[And if with a virgin who is manumitted.]

11. If anyone lies with a virgin who is manumitted, let him compensate with eight solidi to her relatives or to her lord.

[If with another's maidservant.]

12. If anyone lies with another's married maidservant, let him compensate with twenty solidi to her lord.

[If with a virgin maidservant.]

13. If he lies with a virgin maidservant, let him compensate with four solidi.

[If he dismisses his own wife.]

14. If any freeman dismisses his wife, a freewoman, without any fault except his dislike, let him compensate with forty-eight solidi to her relatives. However, let him pay the woman her lawful morning gift according to her status, and whatever she brings with her from her relatives' property, let all those things be returned to the woman.

[If he does not receive his betrothed.]

L. Alam. LII.   15. If any freeman, after he has betrothed himself to someone's daughter (who lawfully is a freewoman), dismisses her and takes another contrary to law, let him compensate with twenty-four solidi to her relatives, and let him swear with twelve oathtakers selected from his own family that he does not dismiss her through dislike for her relatives or for any crime, but takes another because of love for the other. And let it be ended between them, and afterwards let him [her father] give his daughter to whom he wishes.

[If he abducts another's betrothed.]

16. If anyone abducts someone's betrothed or through persua-   L. Alam. LI.
sion takes her for himself as a wife, let him return her and compensate with eighty solidi.

[If he deceives (a woman with) a promise.]

17. If anyone persuades a freewoman as if he meant to marry
her and dismisses her on the way, which the Bavarians call
wancstodal,[64] let him compensate with twelve solidi.

[Concerning an abortion by a potion.]

18. If any woman gives a drink [to a woman] so that she
causes an abortion, if it is a maidservant, let her receive 200 lashes,
and if it is a freewoman, let her lose her freedom and be assigned
to slavery to whomever the duke orders.

[Various cases of abortion.]

19. If anyone causes an abortion in a woman through any blow,   L. Alam. LXX.
if the woman dies, let it be considered the same as a homicide.
However, if the child alone is killed, let him compensate twenty[65]
solidi if the child does not come forth alive. If, however, it was
living [at the time of the abortion], let him pay the wergeld.[66]

[Concerning wergeld (for abortions).]

20. If he causes an abortion, in the first place let him be compelled to pay twelve solidi. Then let him and his posterity pay a
single solidus each year, that is, in the autumn, until the seventh
generation from father to son. And if there is neglect of a single
year, then let him be compelled again to pay twelve solidi and in
turn follow the arrangement described above until the numbered
sequence is completed.

[Concerning the prolonged mortification of the relatives.]

21. Therefore our ancestors have declared an unceasing compensation, and this was decreed after the Christian religion was
established in the world, since after a soul receives flesh, if it does
not come to light of birth, it suffers unceasing punishment, and

without the sacrament of baptism—owing to the abortion—the soul is delivered up to Hell.

[*Concerning an abortion by weakness.*]

22. If, however, a maidservant is weakened by another, in whatever way, so that he causes an abortion, if a child does not come forth alive, let him compensate with four solidi.

[*Concerning an abortion in a maidservant, (let him compensate) as above.*]

23. If, however, it was living [at the time of the abortion], let him compensate with ten solidi; let the maidservant be returned to her lord.

IX.

Concerning theft.

[*If a freeman commits a theft.*]

1. If any freeman steals something, let him compensate for any kind of property ninefold, that is, let him restore nine times.

[*If he steals from a church.*]

L.   Alam.   VI;
          XXXI.

2. And if he steals something from a church, a courtyard of the duke, or a workshop or mill, let him compensate thrice ninefold, that is, let him restore three times nine, since these four houses are public buildings and are always open. And if he wishes to make denial, let him swear according to the value of the property. If he steals one saiga, that is, three denarii, let him swear alone according to his law. If two saigae, that is, six denarii, or even up to one solidus, which equals three tremisses, let him swear with one oathtaker. And if he steals more than one solidus, or three solidi or even up to five solidi, let him swear with six oathtakers. If he steals a domesticated ox or a milk cow which is giving milk, let him swear with six oathtakers, or let the two champions fight, and let the one be chosen to whom God gives strength.[67]

[*If he steals more valuable property.*]

3.[68] And if he steals more valuable property, that is, worth twelve solidi or more, or a horse of the same price or a slave, and he wishes to deny it, let him swear with twelve oathtakers from his kindred or let two champions fight on that account.

[*If he abducts a freeman.*]

4. If any freeman abducts and sells a freeman and he is con-
victed, let him bring him back and restore his freedom and let him compensate for him with forty[69] solidi. However, let him pay forty solidi to the state on account of the presumption that he assumed. And if he cannot bring him back, then let the thief lose his freedom if he cannot pay the wergeld to the relatives, since he delivered up[70] a fellow freeman into slavery.[71] And let nothing more be required.

L. Alam. XLV.

[*If a slave abducts a freeman.*]

5. If, however, a slave abducts and sells a freeman, let his master present him bound before the judge. Let his punishment be in the power of the duke; either let him lose his hands or his eyes. Let him never escape without a mark, although he is a favorite with his master. And if the master commands this or consents to it, let him be subjected to the above sentence, and let him lose[72] that slave.

[*A thief taken in the act of theft at night.*]

6. If a thief is killed in an act of theft at night while he carries stolen property, let no complaint arise from this homicide.

[*If he persuades another's slave to steal.*]

7. If anyone persuades another's slave to steal or cause some injury to his master, so that one can accuse him, and that crime is discovered by the investigation of the judges, let the master neither lose the slave nor suffer any harm through a compensation, but let him by whose provocation the crime is committed be condemned as a thief. Let him compensate ninefold so that the slave is not compelled to pay. But let the slave return what he took, and let him publicly receive 200 lashes of the whip besides.

[*If he buys something from a thief unknowingly.*]

8. If anyone unknowingly buys from a thief, let him seek out the seller after a period of time; if he cannot find him, let him

prove himself innocent with an oath and witnesses. And what is discovered in his possession, let him restore half, and let him not delay to seek the thief. But if he wishes to conceal the thief through perjury, and thereafter it is found out, then let him be condemned for the crime just like that thief.

[*If gold or other kinds of property.*]

9. If anyone steals gold, silver, draft animals, cattle, or whatever property, up to a value of ten solidi or more, and he is convicted, then let the thief when arrested be delivered up to a judge, and let him be subjected to punishment according to law, and let him compensate singly to him who suffered loss. Nevertheless, let him not be condemned to death before he has compensated directly from his property.

[*If he secretly kills another's animal.*]

10. If anyone secretly kills another's horse, ox, or any animal during the night or day and denies it, and afterwards he is convicted, let him compensate for it as if it were stolen.

[*If he accidentally kills another's animal.*]

11. If anyone accidentally kills another's animal and does not deny it, let him not delay to give one of equal value, and let him receive the dead body.

[*Concerning bells.*]

12. If anyone steals a bell from a horse or an ox, let him compensate with one solidus; if from a cow, let him compensate with two tremisses; if from smaller livestock, let him compensate with one tremissis.

[*Concerning gardens.*]

13. If anyone secretly enters into another's garden, let him compensate with three solidi, and what he takes there, let him compensate according to the law as stolen. In the same way the law is to be observed concerning orchards.

[*Concerning the purchase of stolen property.*]

14. Let no one attempt to acquire stolen property within the province. First let him inquire whether or not what he wishes to acquire is stolen.

[*The same as above.*]

15. If he attempts to buy stolen property, and he is convicted, and he does this knowingly, then let him give property of similar value to him whose property he acquired, and let him owe twelve solidi to the public treasury as a *fredus*.

[*Concerning the custody of stolen property.*]

16. Similarly, he who obtains custody of stolen property from the hand of a thief, as if consenting to a theft, let him compensate as we said above, or let him swear with one oathtaker that he did not know that it was stolen when he acquired it or when he obtained it into his custody. There is to be one law for him who buys stolen property and for him who receives it into his custody. However, if he who receives stolen property into his custody refuses to seek out the owner, that man is a thief as if he stole it. And let him compensate as the law states.

[*Concerning compensation from a thief.*]

17. Let no one dare to obtain compensation from a thief in a proven case of theft, unless he [the thief] is sentenced before his judge. If, however, he attempts to do this and hides this from his judge, then let him be subject to the punishment of a thief.

[*Oaths are not to be given hastily.*]

18. Oaths are not to be given hastily. Let a judge know his case well, and [let him inquire] in accordance with the truth beforehand, so that the truth cannot be hidden from him; also, do not let anyone take oaths too readily. However, we wish this to be always observed among the Bavarians, so that a case is investigated and truth arrived at in the presence of a judge. It is not allowed for anyone to judge by himself, but let him be compelled to pay as it is resolved. However, let oaths be allowed in those cases in which a judge finds no proof in an inquiry.

[*Concerning false testimony.*]

19. If anyone testifies falsely against another's life or brings forth a false accusation through some kind of hate, let him receive the punishment or fine that he brings upon the other. Let no one be condemned before you inquire into the truth; it is written: "Prove all things; cling to that which is good."[73]

[*Concerning the accusing of another's slave.*]

20. If anyone accuses another's slave unjustly and tortures him when he is innocent, let him not delay to return a similar slave to his master because he tortured an innocent man. If, however, an innocent man dies under torture, let him restore two slaves of the same value without delay. If he has no slave or cannot compensate, let him be subjected to slavery, since he allowed an innocent man to be killed.

X.

Concerning the burning of houses and their compensation.

[*Concerning setting fire by night.*]

L. Alam.
LXXVI, 1.

1. If anyone sets someone's property on fire through hatred[74] during the night and burns the house of a freeman or slave, in the first place, let him compensate for and restore all of the buildings according to the status of the person, and let him restore each of the furnishings, whatever he burned there. And let him compensate each freeman who escapes naked from that blaze with his *revavunti*.[75] For women, however, let it be double. Then let him compensate for the roof of the house with forty solidi.

[*Concerning the storehouses of freemen.*]

L. Alam.
LXXVI, 2.

2. Concerning the storehouses of freemen. If they are enclosed with walls and are secured with bolts and a key, let him compensate for a roof with twelve solidi. If, however, it is not enclosed, but one which the Bavarians call *scof*, without walls, let him compensate with six solidi. Concerning the granary, which they call *parch*,[76] let him compensate with four[77] solidi. Concerning stacks of grain, if uncovered or burned, let him compensate with three solidi. Concerning lesser buildings, which they

call *scopar,* let him compensate with one solidus, and let him restore all equally.

[*Concerning the knocking down of roofs of buildings.*]

3. Concerning lesser buildings. If anyone destroys or knocks down a roof, which often occurs, or burns it, which they call *firstfalli,* let him compensate with three solidi for each no matter how it is constructed, that is, a bakery, bath, kitchen or other of this kind, and let him restore what he destroyed or burned.

[*Concerning the setting and extinguishing of fires.*]

4. However, if he starts a fire in a house so that the flame bursts forth, and it is not burned down and is saved by the domestic slaves, let him compensate for each one of the freemen with his *hrevavunta,*[78] since he did those things in *inunuuam,*[79] which they say endangers life, and let him not compensate further except for what the fire consumed. However, let the punishment of the duke remain permanent. And if he wishes to deny these things, let him defend himself with a champion, or let him swear with twelve oathtakers. Concerning slaves, however, let each one compensate the *firstfalli* so that a hand is cut off.

[*Concerning the destruction of houses.*]

5. Now, that (we believe) the regulation concerning burning of houses is concluded, it is not inconsistent that we explain the destruction of houses and the compensation of buildings.

[*Concerning roofs.*]

6. If anyone in order to cause abandonment or some other outcome, through presumption or enmity, or even through negligence or stupidity, knocks down a freeman's roof, let him compensate with forty solidi to the owner of the house.

[*Concerning the posts of roofs.*]

7. If he [knocks down] a post by which the roof is held up, which they call *firstsul,* let him compensate with twelve solidi.

[*Concerning inside corner posts.*]

8. If he knocks down that post on the inside of a building which they call *winchilsul,* let him compensate with six solidi.

[*Concerning (other posts) of this type.*]

9. However, let the rest of this type be compensated with three solidi.

[*Concerning outside corner (posts).*]

10. However, for an outside corner post of this type let him compensate with three solidi.

[*Concerning other (posts) of this type.*]

11. For other posts of this type, let him compensate for each with a single solidus.

[*Concerning beams.*]

12. However, let him compensate for all beams with three solidi.

[*Concerning outer (beams), which hold the walls together.*]

13. However, for outer beams, which we call *spanga,* since this type holds the walls together, let him compensate with three solidi.

[*Concerning other buildings.*]

14. However, for the rest, that is, lath, bricks, planks, or whatever is used in buildings, let him compensate for each with a single solidus. And if one person commits all these acts on another's building, let him not be compelled to pay more than for the destruction of the roof or for those crimes greater than this crime. Do not punish minor crimes committed by this person except for making full restoration according to law.

[*Concerning a courtyard.*]

15. If a freeman destroys or breaks into a[80] courtyard, let him compensate with three [solidi][81] and repair the damage.

[*Concerning an outside fence.*]

16. If he breaks or destroys that fence which they call *ezziscgun,*[82] let him compensate with one solidus and restore.

[*Concerning a top pole (of a fence).*]

17. However, for a top pole, [which][83] they call *etorcartea,* which gives stability to a fence, let him compensate in an equal manner if he unjustly cuts it through, since a fence in this condition is least able to sustain an onrush of animals.

[*Concerning signs.*]

18. However, whoever removes or unjustly cuts down a sign which they call *wiffam,* which is placed according to ancient custom for the purpose of defence, either to close an illegal route or to secure or enlarge pasture, let him compensate with one solidus.

[*Concerning a public road.*]

19. If anyone closes a public road, where the king or duke passes by, or a similar road to someone contrary to law, let him compensate with twelve solidi and remove that fence. And if he wishes to deny it, let him swear with twelve oathtakers.

[*Concerning a side road.*]

20. Concerning a side road or a pastoral route from which someone is obstructed by another, let him [the doer] compensate with six solidi and open it, or let him swear with six oathtakers.

[*Concerning a footpath.*]

21. Concerning a footpath which is closed [to someone],[84] let him [the doer] compensate with three solidi, or let him swear with one oathtaker.

[*Concerning a stream.*]

22. If by any way whatever one contaminates or pollutes a stream through any uncleanliness,[85] first let him clean it, so that there is no trace of contamination, and let him compensate with six solidi, or let him swear with six oathtakers.

[*The same as above.*]

23. If, however, a well is polluted by several in a neighborhood, let them divide the compensation among themselves; moreover, let them restore the well to its former condition.

XI.

Concerning violence.

[*Concerning a courtyard.*]

L. Alam. XCIV,
2.
1. If anyone enters another's courtyard by force contrary to law, let him compensate with three solidi.

[*Concerning a house (if a man enters it by force).*]

2. If, however, he forcibly enters a house and finds nothing there of his own, let him compensate with six solidi.

[*As above (a warning against forcible entry).*]

3. Indeed, let no one forcibly enter another's house, since this creates a dispute.

[*In a similar manner (after the entrant has been judged guilty).*]

4. And after he enters and confesses his guilt that he entered unjustly, let him give a pledge to the owner of the house; and if the owner is absent, let him place that pledge upon the threshold, and let him not be compelled to pay more than three solidi.

5.[86] Whoever resists [a search] of his house, which they call *selisohan,* let him compensate for such property [since] he withheld examination. [Let him compensate with] forty solidi to the state. This is decreed.

6. Whoever does not wish to acknowledge property taken by theft, which they call *zauganzuht,* let him compensate as stolen. This is decreed.

7. Whoever resists a seizure, which they call *hantalod,*[87] let him pay forty solidi to the state and return the property sought, or other similar property. This is decreed.

XII.

Concerning the knocking down of boundary markers.

[*Concerning boundary lines.*]

1. If anyone dares to level boundary lines or remove fixed boundary markers, let him compensate, if he is a freeman, with six solidi for each sign or marker in the neighborhood.

[If a slave does this.]

2. If [he is][88] a slave, let him receive fifty lashes of the whip for each sign.

[Concerning a boundary (accidentally leveled).]

3. If anyone accidentally levels a boundary marker, while he plows or plants a vineyard, let him restore the marker to its original location, and let him incur no loss.

[Concerning disputes over boundary markers.]

4. However often a dispute occurs concerning boundary markers, it is necessary[89] to examine signs that were set in place in ancient times, that is, a mound of earth that apparently was heaped up in former times for an earthen boundary, or stones that were set up as obvious evidence in the form of distinguishable chiseled boundary markers. If these signs are lacking, then it is fitting to consider markers on trees, which they call *decorvas*,[90] if those can be proved to have been cut in former times. But if, perhaps, one possesses a portion [of land] for some time within a stranger's boundary markers through the absence or ignorance of the owner, let him lose this immediately to the owner, as soon as the ancient and recognizable boundaries are discerned by the inspectors. Do not let him acquire possession of [land within] recognizable markers for any long period of time, unless he acquired it from someone; then let him present the seller, and let him define according to law.

[Concerning the prohibition of new boundary markers.]

5. Let no one set up a new boundary marker without consent of the other party or without an inspector.

[If a freeman does this.]

6. If, on the one hand, a freeman does this, let him incur the fine for trespassing that is contained in the laws, that is, six solidi.

[*If a slave does this.*]

7. If, however, a slave commits this act without the knowledge of his master, let him receive, stretched out publicly, 200 lashes of the whip, and let no blame be attached to his master from this.

[*Concerning unrecognizable markers.*]

L. Alam.
LXXXI.

8. However often a dispute arises over common markers, where recognizable markers do not appear in trees, mountains, or rivers, and one man says, "My ancestors held this land as far as this point and bequeathed it to me in full ownership," let him indicate the place according to his own claim. Nevertheless, let the other enter this land, and let him indicate the other place that he claimed previously he and his ancestors had always held up to the present. And if proof cannot be found, and both parties do not wish to compromise the breach, then let them respond in turn with what they call *wehadinc,* and let the fighters not draw lots, but let God give strength and victory to the one the designated portion of the disputed territory belongs to.

[*Concerning the laying of beams (that is, the hasty construction of a building).*]

9. If anyone wishes to construct a building quickly [and illegally] before a dispute is settled, and on the other hand, another party objects to its hasty construction and from that time has a witness, and he [the claimant] stubbornly does not wish to comply with the law, but finishes his house and secures the buildings by enclosing them with a fence, and then says, "Leave my land, since I am within the law"; and the possessor says to the contrary that he has possession and should not leave, and [the possessor] says, "I have a witness who can prove the hasty construction of your building," then let the witness swear, give evidence, and let the decision be determined by fighters.

[*Concerning other (buildings) of this kind.*]

10. Concerning other buildings of this kind and enclosures, let him by no means give evidence, but let him who built them defend himself according to the law. However, if a courtyard is not enclosed, let him who wishes to defend himself throw at midday an ax worth a saiga to the east and to the west. To the north let him

lay down a fence no further than the shadow extends, unless the dispute is settled.⁹¹

[*Concerning lumber that is not (yet) removed.*]

11. If anyone cuts or damages someone's lumber in the forest, because of either enmity or envy, let him give other lumber of equal value, and let him compensate with one solidus.

12.⁹² And if he takes lumber for his own use, let him not make restitution with the other party except through a settlement, and let him compensate with one solidus for as long as he retains the lumber.

XIII.

Concerning pledges.

[*Let no one be allowed to pledge.*]

1. Let no one be allowed to pledge except through an order of the judge. If some man, perhaps, is so harsh, [or]⁹³ disobedient, or defiantly rebellious of justice that he refuses to respond legally and render justice, that man is a despiser of the law; such a person is to be restrained by the judge.

[*Concerning one who refuses to render justice.*]

2. If any freeman refuses to render justice to another freeman who summons him concerning any matter whatever, let him who pleads his case have two or three witnesses there who heard and saw what the other replied, so that they can act as witnesses before the judge. Then let the judge order him to come into his presence, and judge him, and let that man compensate twelve solidi since he did not wish to give justice to him to whom he owed it. Thus, let him compensate with twelve solidi for the trouble he caused the one who originally summoned him, since he did not wish to give justice to one who deserved it, no matter what he was summoned for. And afterwards let him answer to the law and render justice as the law requires. Moreover, [let him compensate with] forty solidi to the duke as a *fredus*.

[*If he accepts a pledge contrary to law.*]

3. If anyone accepts a pledge contrary to law, without the duke's order, let him return the pledge unharmed, and let him add another

equal in value; however, [let him compensate with] forty solidi to the duke as a *fredus*. And if he harms that pledge, let him compensate as much as it is appraised by him who judges the case. Indeed, this should not occur, since it causes a dispute, and for every pledge he accepts contrary to law, let him always compensate with six solidi. If that pledge is worth less than six solidi, then let him return the pledge and compensate with six solidi. And if, however, the pledge he accepts is worth more than six solidi, let him return that pledge unharmed and add another equal in value. However, [let him compensate with] forty solidi to the duke as a *fredus*.

[*If he accepts pigs as a pledge.*]

L. Alam. XCIV, 4.

4. If anyone accepts pigs as a pledge contrary to law, let him compensate for each one with two saigae. Let him compensate for a breeding sow with one tremissis.

[*If he offers sheep as a pledge.*]

L. Alam. XCIV, 4.

5. If anyone offers sheep as a pledge contrary to law, let him keep silent concerning the case for which he offers the pledge, and let him compensate with one solidus, unless it so happens that the man has no other property to offer as a pledge; if he does not have property except these sheep, let him not be liable, since necessity forced him to do this.

[*If he plows another's crops or meadow.*]

6. If anyone plows another's crops or meadow with a yoke up to three [furrows] in length or six furrows in width, let him compensate with three solidi. And if he wishes to deny it, let him swear with one oathtaker.

[*If he steals a ripe crop.*]

7. If anyone steals a crop already ripe in the field, let him compensate with six solidi. And if he wishes to deny it, let him swear with six oathtakers according to the law.

[*If he performs (magic on) another's crops.*]

8. If anyone performs magic on another's crops through witchcraft, which they call *aranscarti,* and he is discovered, let him com-

pensate with twelve solidi. And let him [the latter] have the former's domestic slaves and all his property and livestock in his care for a year. And if that man loses any of these things in that year, let him make restitution. And if he wishes to deny it, let him swear with twelve oathtakers, or let him defend himself with a girded fighter, that is, by wager of battle [trial by combat].

[*If he persuades a slave to flee.*]

9. If anyone persuades another's slave to flee and leads him outside the boundary, that is, beyond the borders, let him compensate with twelve solidi and bring him back. And if he wishes to deny it, let him swear with twelve oathtakers or seek his justice with fighters. If it is a maidservant, let him compensate with twenty-four solidi and return her.

XIV.

Concerning injuries to animals and their compensation.

[*Concerning injuries to animals.*]

1. [If animals] which cause damage to a fence and are accustomed to this habit hurt themselves on a post while leaving or entering, and they die as a result of this, if the fence is legally constructed, that is, the average stature of a man up to his chest, let the owner of the fence not be forced to pay any compensation.

[*Concerning him who drives it into a fence.*]

2. If another person deliberately drives[94] the animal [into a fence], let him pay for the animal since he unjustly brought it into danger of death.

[*If the owner of the fence does this.*]

3. If the owner of a fence in a similar manner drives out [an animal] from his enclosures with dogs or thrashing, let him compensate similarly.

[*If it does not die (immediately).*]

4. If, however, it does not die immediately and escapes injured to the house of its owner, and the owner of the animal learns of

this, let him say to the party who drove this animal to death, "Receive the animal which you have injured," which we call *avursam*.[95]

[*If he confesses, let him receive it.*]

5. If, moreover, he confesses to this crime, let him receive [the animal] until it is healed, and during this time let him bring it back to health, as it was when he injured it.

[*Concerning the restoration of animals.*]

6. If, however, it dies, let the possessor keep the animal that he injured. Let him keep for his own use the carcass that he was unable to heal.

[*If he does not wish to receive the injured animal.*]

7. If, however, he does not wish[96] to receive the animal he injured, let the owner of the animal receive the carcass for his use, and let the possessor nevertheless be compelled to pay in full.

[*If he knocks out an eye from another's animal.*]

8. [12.][97] If anyone knocks out an eye from someone's horse, ox, or any four-footed animal, let him appraise what the beast is worth and compensate a third part.

[*If a horn from an ox.*]

9. If anyone knocks off a horn from the head of another's ox, let him compensate with one tremissis; if he knocks out a horn and a bone remains, let him give two saigae.

[*If from a cow.*]

10. If he knocks a horn from a cow, let him compensate two saigae.

[*If he cuts off a tail (from a horse).*]

L. Alam.
LXIII, 1.   11. If he cuts off a tail or an ear, if it is a horse which we call *marhc*,[98] let him compensate with one solidus.

[*Concerning (a horse) of average value. (Concerning a horse) of inferior value.*[99]]

12. If it is of average value, which they call *wilz,* let him compensate with one-half solidus. And if it is of inferior value, which we call *angargnago,* which is unsuitable for military campaigns, let him compensate with one tremissis.

L. Alam. LXIII, 2.

13. Similarly, let him who cuts a tail or an ear from another's ox compensate with one tremissis.

[*Concerning (the injuring of) a cow in this way.*]

14. If he injures another's cow in this way, let him compensate with two saigae.

[*Concerning unjust treatment (of animals).*]

15. And if he hurts one of these contrary to law, which we call *suezcholi,* let him be subject to an equal punishment.

[*The same as above.*]

16. And if any defiant person does an injustice to another's draft animal because of contempt for or hatred of the owner, let its total value be compensated doubly.

[*Let no one attempt to kill another's animal.*]

17. Let no one attempt to kill another's animal, not even a pig, although it may have caused him damage; let him confine it until he shows the damage to its owner, and let some of the neighbors see this, and let them indicate the place that is damaged and another place that is untouched so that the harvest can be reaped. And however much loss he finds in the damaged place, let him whose animal caused the damage make full compensation. Let him also compensate similarly for vineyards and meadows. As the appraisers decide, let it be compensated.

L. Alam. LXVII, 2.

XV.

Concerning commendation and contracts.

[*Concerning custody.*]

1. If anyone entrusts a horse or any kind of animal into another's custody at a prearranged price, and it dies, let him who

received the animal into his care pay for one of equal value, even if he complied with the price of the custody. But if he did not receive it at a prearranged price, and it can be shown to be dead, let him neither pay the price of that animal nor let any other thing be required of him. Nevertheless, it is reasonable for him who received an animal entrusted to him to take an oath that it was not[100] through his fault or carelessness that the animal died, and let him return the hide. Let the same regulation also be observed for borrowing.

[*If he steals gold.*]

2. If anyone entrusts or hands over gold, silver, ornaments, or anything to be placed in custody or on sale, and, perhaps, these things together with his own property in his house are consumed by a fire, let him who received them into his custody take an oath with witnesses that it has not served to his advantage, and let him not be forced to return anything except gold and silver, which cannot be burned.

[(*If he steals*) *from a fire in this way.*]

3. If anyone enters a house while it is consumed by flames as if to bring help and, perhaps, steals something, let the owner of the house inquire conscientiously. And if he can find him who stole any property, let the thief return what he stole fourfold. And if, perhaps, one finds any entrusted property with the plunderer, let him not delay to return it to the owner.[101]

[*Concerning the stealing of entrusted property.*]

4.[102] If, however, the things that are entrusted are proven to have been seized by theft, let a period of time be allowed to him who lost this entrusted property until he discovers the thief through investigation. And if he finds him, let him return only this particular property to the owner. Compensation, moreover, belongs to him who lost entrusted property by theft.

[*Concerning regulations* (*pertaining to a thief within a reasonable period*) *of time.*]

5. And if a thief is not found within a reasonable period of time, let half the entrusted property [remaining] be returned to the

owner who should keep it; however, let both maintain half the loss. And if afterwards the owner finds in the hands of him who entrusted it anything concealed, whereas the latter said previously that he had lost it or that it was taken through theft, the law declares that this is to be treated as a theft. Let him be compelled to pay the compensation.

[*Concerning property contested in a dispute.*]

6. It is not allowed to give away or sell property contested in a dispute.

[*Concerning widows.*]

7. Concerning widows. Let her who remains in widowhood after the death of her husband have a portion in usufruct equal to her sons', that is, as if she were one of the sons. For as long as she lives, let her legally possess it by right of usufruct.

[*Concerning second marriages.*]

8. But if a mother contracts another marriage, on that day let the sons who are born of the earlier marriage take over her portion of the usufruct[103] from her husband's property, whatever remains of the paternal inheritance. However, let a mother depart if she has her own property, [with][104] her morning gift, which she possesses legally. And if she has borne neither sons nor daughters [from her former marriage], let everything she took away from [the late husband's] children [that is, those of a former marriage] be returned to them after his death.

[*Concerning division among brothers.*]

9. Let brothers divide the inheritance of their father equally. If he [the father] had many wives and all were freewomen of his class, but not equally wealthy, let each son possess the inheritance of his mother. Moreover, let the paternal inheritance be divided equally. If, however, he has sons by a maidservant, let them not receive a portion with their brothers, except as much as their brothers wish to give them through charity, since it has been written in the Old Testament, "A son of a maidservant is not an heir with a son of a freewoman."[105] Nevertheless, they should exercise mercy, since these are of his own flesh.

L. Alam.
LXXXV.

[*Concerning him who dies without children.*]

10. Concerning him who dies without sons and daughters. Let a wife keep her portion as long as she is provided by her widowhood, that is, half the property; however, let half belong to the relatives of the husband. If, however, the wife dies or takes another husband, then let him keep what is his own and what was to be given to her from the property of the husband according to the law. Let the relatives of the former husband keep the remaining property. If, however, her husband has neither sons, daughters, grandchildren, great-grandchildren, nor any near relatives, but bestows upon his wife, through gift or will, either part or all of his property, and she remains in widowhood all this time and guards the memory of her husband with modest chastity, let her possess all those things which were given to her by her husband, and let her transfer them to whomever she wishes in her own right. But if the husband and wife die without heirs, and no one is found even to the seventh degree, and they do not have any relatives at all, then let the public treasury acquire these properties.[106]

XVI.

Concerning sales.

[*If one sells another's property.*]

1.[107] If anyone sells another's property without consent of the owner, either a slave or maidservant or anything whatever, let him return it according to law, and let him add another of equal value. And if he cannot recover it, let him return two of equal value.

[*If he sells a possession.*]

2. If anyone sells to another his possession, that is, arable land, waste land, meadows, or forests, after reception of the purchase price, either through a charter or through witnesses, let the purchase be considered legally valid. The witness should be heard orally, since our law requires it; two or three ought to be [witnesses].[108] If a sale is concluded forcibly, that is, settled by threat of death or by fear of restraint, at no time is it legally valid.

[*If one acquires something from another's slave.*]

3. If anyone acquires something from another's slave without the knowledge of his owner, if the owner does not wish to vali-

date[109] the purchase, the purchase is to be returned; the purchase is not legally valid. If he [the receiver] does not have it himself, let him return one of equal value.

[*Concerning a dispute over acquired property.*]

4. Whenever a dispute arises concerning the sale of property, if it is established that it is another's, let it not be acquired without the owner's consent. And let him who attempts to sell another's property be compelled to pay twofold to the owner; nevertheless, let the purchase price be returned to the buyer who acquired it. And let whatever is added for the improvement of the property by the buyer for his own advantage be appraised by the judges of that region, and let a fair price [be rendered][110] by the seller to him who is known to have improved the property.

[*If one sells a freeman.*]

5. If anyone sells a freeman while he has his freedom, let him who sells him bring him back to the place of capture and restore the liberty to him which he had before, and let him compensate him with forty solidi. In addition, let him be compelled to pay to the buyer twice the purchase price he received. Similarly, twofold [compensation] is to be observed concerning women. And if he sells him, and [the latter] cannot be brought back, then let him compensate with the wergeld, that is, let him pay 160 solidi to the relatives.

L. Alam. XLV; XLVI.

[*If (he sells) his own slaves.*]

6. If anyone sells his slave, perhaps not knowing what property he has, let his master who sold him have the power of reclaiming those properties wherever he can find them.

[*If a slave buys his freedom with his own property.*]

7. If any [slave][111] buys his freedom with his property, and perhaps his master does not know this, let him not pass from the power of his master, since his master unknowingly received not the purchase price but the property of his slave.

[*Concerning an exchange.*]

8. Let an exchange, that is, what they call *campias*,[112] have the same validity as a purchase.

[Concerning the form of a sale.]

9. This form of sale is to be observed, whether property, slaves, or any kind of animal is sold, so that no one may break a legally valid sale, that is, property sold at a set price. But after the sale is transacted, it is not to be changed, unless it happens that one finds a defect (that it is either blind, ruptured, epileptic, or leprous), which the seller concealed in it, that is, in a slave or a horse or whatever sort of animal. In animals, however, there are defects that the seller can often conceal. If, however, the seller states the defect, let the sale stand; one cannot change it. If, however, he does not state it, one can change it on this day, on the next, and on the third day. And if one has his property for more than three nights, after this he cannot change it, unless perhaps he cannot find the defect in three days. Then, when he finds it, let him [the seller] take back the property he sold defectively. Or if he does not wish to take it back, let him swear with one oathtaker, "I know of no defect in it on that day when we transacted the sale"; and let the bargain stand.

[Concerning earnest money.]

10. What earnest money he gave for any property, let him be compelled to pay in full the purchase price that is pleasing to the buyer. And if he does not come on the established day, or does not ask before this for more time, and he neglects to do this, then let him lose the earnest money and pay in full the purchase price that he owed.

[Concerning the affirmation (of sales).]

11. And let him say variously concerning a slave, "I seized [that][113] slave outside the border where the duke led his army," and in other circumstances, "The duke acquired him by way of a fair and just debt, and he was given to me freely," or concerning other ornaments, "These things are manufactured by my slave from my own material or by my smith," if they are of this type. "Therefore I brought them and I confirm them." If these confirmations are lacking in the elements mentioned above, by no means can he affirm [ownership of] them. If, however, he confirms them, he cannot get them back from him to whom he confirmed them, unless that man [the latter] wishes it, provided that the fighter of the plaintiff wins.

[*The same as above.*]

12. If he promises the buyer to confirm this, that is *suiron,* and he cannot truthfully state the words that we said above, and breaks the arrangement, then let him return the purchase price and restore such land or property as he promised to confirm without delay, since it is very reprehensible to give another's property, because disputes often arise over this.

[*The same as above.*]

13. In a similar manner [let it be observed regarding him] who gives away to another his own property that he associated with himself [but] never held, because of an illegal act.

[*In a similar manner.*]

14. If it is a slave, let one say, "My father willed him to me in my inheritance," or "I raised him in my own home; he was born of my own slave." Similarly, let him declare this concerning draft animals or things of that kind.

[*(A sale) is to be confirmed through a charter or witnesses.*]

15. Whatever a man sells or whatever property he buys, let all be confirmed through charters or through witnesses who can prove this, that is, concerning slaves, land, houses, or forests, so that afterwards there is no dispute.

[*Concerning contracts or agreements.*]

16. Concerning contracts or agreements. We insist that contracts or agreements that are made through writing of some sort or through three or more designated witnesses not be altered for any reason, as long as the day and year are clearly indicated on them. L. Alam. XLII, 2.

[*Concerning those who sell their own freehold.*]

17. Concerning those who sell their own freehold[114] or any other property: if another wishes to take this away from the buyer and add it to his property, then let the buyer say to the seller, "My neighbor wishes to take away my land," or whatever property it L. Alam. LXXXI.

is, or whoever it is. And let the other [the seller] answer, "I wish to confirm what I gave you legally and through oral testimony." Let this be done as established above for seven nights. If one says, with both parties convened together, "Why do you attempt to invade my land, which I was given justly according to the law of inheritance?" and the other says to the contrary, "Why do you give away my land, which my ancestors held formerly?" let the other [the seller] say, "This is not true, since my ancestors held it and bequeathed it to me as my freehold, and it is now invested in the hands of him who seized it; I wish to affirm it through the law." If he wishes it, as soon as possible, let him have full power of possession. If not, however, let it be confirmed after three or five days, or perhaps even after seven, in the following manner. At the four corners of the field or at designated boundary markers, let him [the original owner] lift up some ground or circle around with a plow or even, if it is a forest, [seize] grass or twigs, and say these words, "I give this to you, and I confirm it lawfully." Let him say these words three times, and let him hand over [this clod of earth] with his left hand; however, let him offer a pledge to him who summons him with these words, "Behold, I give this pledge to you, that I do not give your land to another in violation of the law." Then let the other receive the pledge and give it to his guarantors, in fulfillment of the law. If the matter between them leads to a fight, let him who received the pledge say, "You have unjustly confirmed my land to another," that is, *farsuirotos*.[115] "You must return it to me and compensate with twelve solidi." Then let them reply with wager of battle, and let the judgment be in the hands of God. If not, however, let him defend himself with an oath, that is, with twelve oathtakers, that he did not confirm land to another unjustly, nor must he restore it to his control, nor must he compensate with twelve solidi.

XVII.

Concerning witnesses and their cases.

[*Concerning witnesses (regarding the entering of another's land).*]

L. Alam.
XCVIII, 1, 2.
1. If any man irregularly enters another's meadow, cultivated land, or clearing contrary to law and says that it is his own, let him compensate with six solidi because of his audacity, and get out.

[*If he wishes to lay his claim.*]

2. If, however, a claimant wishes to lay his claim to that cultivated land, meadow, clearing, or wherever this dispute occurs,
let him lay claim in the following way. Let him swear with six
oathtakers and say, "I have not infringed upon your occupation
there contrary to law, nor ought I to compensate with six solidi or
get out, since my work and labor were previous to yours." Then
let the possessor say, "I have witnesses who know that I have
always done the work of this field; I have plowed, cleared, and
possessed this land to the present day, which no one can contradict, and my father left it to me in his inheritance." The man
who wishes to testify to this ought to be his neighbor and ought
to have six solidi in money and an equal amount in cultivated
land. Then let that witness swear in the following way, "I
have heard with my ears and seen with my eyes that this man's
occupation in this land was previous to yours and that he produced
fruitful labor, [etc.]." After giving the oath, let the possessor return
the land. If he hopes that justice [is upheld][116] concerning this
cultivated land, and this occurs in the presence of the people, that
he not lose anything through hatred, then let that defender say to
that witness: "You swore falsely against me. Answer me by wager
of battle, and let God indicate if you swore falsely [or truthfully][117]
in reply to me, and you ought to compensate me with twelve
solidi and return the land that you took falsely." If he who seeks
the land wins, let him [the possessor] compensate with twelve
solidi and return the land; and if he cannot give the land, let him
give other land in the neighborhood that is as large as that mea-
sured with the throw of an ax worth one saiga. And if he does not
have it in the neighborhood or cannot acquire it, let him swear
according to the value of the land that he cannot acquire this land
at the set price, nor at two- or threefold [the price], and let him
give land where he has it, and let him swear that the land which
he gives is of the same type as his own.

[*If he has a witness with hearsay evidence.*]

3. If anyone has a witness with hearsay evidence concerning any
settled case, and this is confirmed by witnesses, after this he ought
not to seek or annoy that one with whom he settled the case. And
if he wishes, let him defend himself through witnesses. Let the
witnesses testify where the hearsay evidence is derived, and let

L. Alam. XCI.

him confirm this through an oath. His adversary ought not to withhold witnesses from the truth, unless he [the former] wishes to have false witnesses. He can repel his adversary according to law with wager of battle and say, "I do not derive a witness from you in this case nor do I consent to [accept one]." If, however, witnesses are derived through hearsay evidence regarding the arrangement of compensation or concerning earnest money, when he gives a pledge for any thing until he pays the debt and receives the pledge, let no one refuse that witness or be able to, but let him consent to it. If he wishes to testify in some case concerning a homicide, he can contradict this with [wager of battle and say,] "I wish [to defend]¹¹⁸ this with my fighter against what you said, since you and your witness lie concerning this homicide."

[*If he is conquered.*]

4. And if he who wishes to deny witnesses concerning a homicide is conquered, then let him not be allowed to fight a juridical duel any more, since he obtained evidence for a homicide through force. Let him testify with an oath as the law requires, and let the testimony be legally valid.

[*Where there is disagreement among the judges.*]

5. But our judges may disagree concerning a settlement because he who brings witnesses must swear that he does not bring false witnesses, or he must be stopped from taking an oath concerning this evidence.

[*If there are more witnesses.*]

6. And if there are more witnesses, and they come to one assembly, let the witnesses cast lots among themselves. And let him to whom the lot falls swear in the following manner and say, "I am chosen as a witness, and I wish to render as a witness." Let him hold the hand of the nearest person from his party and say, "Let God help him whose hand I hold that I am a witness among you with hearsay evidence, and I speak the truth about this case." Then let him swear alone with his own hand [; afterwards let him give his weapons for consecration, and let him swear his words upon them with one oathtaker].¹¹⁹ And if he swears falsely, let him

compensate to him whose case he harmed. Let him compensate with twelve solidi, and let him make restitution for that case, or let him defend himself with his fighter, that is, by wager of battle, if he swears rightly.

XVIII.

Concerning champions and cases that pertain to them.

[*If one is killed by another.*]

1. If one of these is killed by another, although he is a noble person, let him not be compensated with more than twelve solidi; and let him be compensated by the man who hired him unjustly.

[*If he is a slave.*]

2. If he is a slave [who fought] with the consent of his master, let him be under a similar regulation. [If, however, he fought without consent], let the hirer compensate [him with][120] twenty solidi.

XIX.

Concerning dead men and their compensation.

[*If anyone digs up a dead man from the grave.*]

1. If anyone digs up a dead freeman from a grave, let him compensate with forty solidi to the relatives, and let him compensate for that which he secretly took from there.

L. Alam. **XLIX,** 1.

[*If one throws (a dead man) into a river.*]

2. If anyone kills a freeman in a secret manner and throws him into a river or throws him into such a place that the corpse cannot be recovered, which the Bavarians call *murdrida,* in the first place let him compensate with forty solidi, since he cannot recover the corpse for a worthy burial. After that, however, let him compensate with the wergeld. And if the corpse is cast from the bed of the stream to the bank and is found by someone who throws the body from the bank again, and he is convicted, let him compensate with twelve solidi.

L. Alam. XLVIII.

[*If he is a slave.*]

L. Alam.
XLVIII.

3. If a slave is killed in a secret [way],[121] in the manner described above, and hidden, which they call *camurdrit,* let the doer compensate ninefold, that is, 180 solidi.

[*Concerning the clothing of the dead.*]

L. Alam.
XLVIII.

4. Concerning their clothing: if he takes this from the dead, which they call *valuraupa,*[122] let him compensate twofold; if from another corpse and not from this one, let him compensate all things as if stolen.

[*If he injures a corpse (with an arrow).*]

5. And if, as often happens, eagles and other birds find the corpse, and because of this it is lacerated, and someone shoots an arrow at the bird and injures the corpse instead, and this is discovered, let him compensate with twelve solidi.

[*If one injures a corpse (by other means).*]

6. In a similar manner, let whoever injures a corpse another has killed always compensate with twelve solidi, if he cuts off a head, if he chops off a hand, a foot, an ear, or any injury that we consider capable of producing a bloodfeud, whether for large or small injuries.

[*If he buries a corpse.*]

7. And if a corpse, [be he freeman or slave],[123] is found by someone, and he buries him through human kindness, so that he is neither defiled by pigs nor torn to pieces by wild beasts or dogs, [and afterwards he is discovered],[123] if he who buried him wishes to ask for something, let the relatives pay him one solidus, or the master of the slave, if he was a slave. If he is not discovered, however, let him receive compensation from the Lord, since it is written, "Bury the dead."[124]

[*The same as above.*]

8. Since we frequently see a corpse buried in the earth and a marker erected above it, let the guardian of a corpse, together with all the bystanders, be invited first to throw dirt on it. And if it is a

freeman, it should be a son or brother and not gravediggers, since these may be selected by inequitable judges who are not learned in the old law.

[*Concerning boats.*]

9. If anyone takes another's boat from its place, let him return it unharmed or [return] one equal in value.

[*As above.*]

10. And if he drags it out of the water and hides it, and denies this when questioned, let him compensate for it as stolen.

XX.

Concerning dogs and their compensation.[125]

1. If anyone steals or kills a hunting dog, which they call *leitihunt,*[126] let him return that one or one equal in value and compensate with six solidi. And if he wishes to deny it, let him swear according to his law with three oathtakers. L. Alam. LXXVIII, 1, 3.

2. If, however, he steals a trained hunting dog, which they call *triphunt,* let him compensate with three solidi or swear with one oathtaker. L. Alam. LXXVIII, 1, 3.

3. Whoever steals [a dog] which tracks footprints while being led by a leash, which they call *spurihunt,* let him compensate with six solidi and return one equal in value or that one.

4. Concerning dogs, which they call *piparhunt,* which hunt game under the ground, let him return, if he kills it, one equal in value and compensate with six solidi.

5. Concerning greyhounds that not only chase a rabbit but catch it through swiftness, let him compensate with one equal in value and three solidi. L. Alam. LXXVIII, 4.

6. Concerning a dog which is called *hapuhhunt,* let him be liable for an equal fine.

7. Concerning dogs that chase bears or buffaloes, that is, large wild animals (which they call *suarzwild*),[127] if he kills one of these, let him compensate with one equal in value and six solidi. L. Alam. LXXVIII, 4.

8. However, let whoever kills a sheep dog that catches the wolf compensate with three solidi. L. Alam. LXXVIII, 5.

L. Alam.
LXXVIII, 6.

9. If, however, after sunset, one kills a dog which defends the courtyard of its master, which they call *hovawart,* let him compensate with three solidi as if it was done in theft. If, moreover, he does this while the sun is still shining, let him compensate with one equal in value and one solidus. If, moreover, a dog holds a man by his clothing or a limb, and he strikes it with his hand so that it dies, let him return one equal in value, and let nothing more be required. And let the owner of this dog compensate half its value as if he had done it himself. If he does not wish to do this, let him not require the new dog.[128]

XXI.

Concerning hawks.[129]

L. Alam. XCVI, 1.

1. If someone kills a hawk, which they call *cranohari,*[130] let him compensate with six solidi and one equal in value, and let him swear with one oathtaker that it is of equal value in flying and seizing.

L. Alam. XCVI, 1.

2. For one that is called *canshapuh,* which seizes geese, let him compensate with three solidi and return one equal in value.

3. For the one that we call *anothapuh,* let him compensate with one solidus and one equal in value.

4. Concerning *sparawaris,*[131] however, let him be liable for an equal fine, that is, one solidus, and let him give compensation of equal value and take an oath, saying that they are of equal value to those killed.

5. If, however, they are carried off in theft, let him be compelled to pay for all things as if stolen, as the law requires.

6. Concerning the birds that are domesticated from wild birds by human effort and are tamed so that they can fly and sing in the courtyards of nobles, let him compensate with one solidus and one equal in value, and, in addition, let him take an oath.

XXII.

Concerning orchards and their compensation.[132]

1. If anyone digs up another's orchard through envy or cuts down fruit-bearing trees where there were twelve or more, in the

first place let him compensate forty solidi, twenty of which are for the orchard, and the other twenty for the state, since he acted contrary to law. And let him plant other trees equal in value there, and for each tree let him compensate with one solidus, and let him give one solidus at fruit-bearing season until the trees he planted bear fruit.

2. If anyone cuts down another's bush, let him compensate with one solidus and one equal in value, if it bears fruit and is a berry bush.

3. And if [he cuts down] more up to the number of six, let him give [one solidus][133] for each. Then let him be compelled to replace that many trees, and for each that does not bear fruit, let him [compensate] with one tremissis and restore one equal in value.

4. Concerning beech trees, however, we propose one tremissis [as compensation], and let him restore one equal in value, up to a total of six solidi for all, that is, eighteen trees; and if the owner sustains more loss, let the cutter not be compelled to pay, except to replace the number.

5. For an apple or pear tree or others of this type, let him be liable for the same fine as [the law] already requires.

6. If, however, he cuts branches from a small forest, a grove, or any hedge, let him compensate with one equal in value and one solidus, and let him pay up to [six][134] solidi for restoration and compensation.

7. If there are a greater number of branches, let him not be compelled to compensate, except to replace with those equal in value and take an oath. If, however, after compensation and restoration, he again enters to do damage in the grove for which he compensated, let nothing be excluded from the sentence of compensation, but let the sentence of the above-named regulation be observed.

8. If bees, that is, someone's swarm, escape from the beehive, and land in a tree in another's grove, and [their owner] follows them, then let him call him to whom the tree belongs, and let him drive out his swarm with smoke and three blows of a cross-ax, if he can, so that the tree is not injured. And let what remains belong to the owner of the tree.

9. If, however, bees enter receptacles placed for the capture of bees, that is, beehives, in a similar way, let him call him to whom the hive belongs, and let him strive to drive out his swarm. Nevertheless, let him not open or injure the hive. If it is wood, let him throw it three times on the ground; if it is held together by bark [or by wicker wood, let him strike the hive three times with his fist][135] and no more. And the bees that are driven out are his, and those that remain belong to him who owns the hive.

10. If, however, he does not inform the owner of the trees or hives, and brings back the swarm to his own property without his [the latter's] knowledge, and the owner of the hive compels him to return them from his own hive or tree and to make restoration, which they call *untprut,* and if that other one wishes to deny it and says that he followed his own swarm, then let him swear with six oathtakers that he did not unjustly bring his swarm from his [the other's] hive, nor ought he to compensate for this according to the judgment.

11. In a similar manner, retribution is established concerning birds, so that no one attempts to take birds from another's forest even though he finds them first, unless he is his neighbor [that is, a fellow landholder], which we call *calasneo.* And [if][136] another attempts this, we demand that he always take an oath of restitution for any injustice. Although a complaint may often be unimportant, [the law][136] compels one to swear with six oathtakers.

XXIII.

Concerning pigs.[137]

1. If anyone drives out or disperses a freeman's pigs by means of a shout or noise [in a place] where there are seventy-two pigs and the herdsman carries a pig's horn, let him compensate with twelve solidi.[138]

NOTES

Prologue

[1] The divine laws are the Ten Commandments.

[2] The name "Soron" is an error. Reference should be to Draco, Athenian archon (or chief magistrate), who framed laws known for their severity in 621 B.C.

[3] Mercurius Trimegistus is a curious name meaning "a messenger performing three functions within the pharaoh's court." It probably describes Ahmose (or Amasis), an Egyptian marshal, who became pharaoh in 569 B.C. and revised the laws. He died in 525 B.C., just before the Persian conquest of Egypt. Solon (see n. 4 below) visited Ahmose during his ten-year absence from Athens.

[4] Solon, who was archon of Athens from 594–93 B.C., drafted a new constitution for Athens in 594 B.C., which laid the foundation of Athenian democracy in subsequent years.

[5] Ligurgus (Lycurgus), sometimes seen as a legendary figure, promulgated the laws of Sparta ca. 885 B.C. His laws were not written down but committed to memory.

[6] Although Numa Pompilius is believed to have written several books of law, their authenticity is greatly disputed. He was a Sabine who became king of Rome during 715–672 B.C. and is credited with introducing Roman religious institutions.

[7] The legendary hero Romulus is credited with founding the city of Rome in 753 B.C. Roma (Rome) is derived from his name.

[8] The laws of the Twelve Tables were promulgated in 451–49 B.C. They constitute the earliest code of Roman law.

[9] Gnaeus Pompeius (d. 48 B.C.), more commonly known as Pompey, became consul in 70 B.C. and was a member of the triumvirate during the Roman Civil War. He became Julius Caesar's rival for power between the Roman Senate and aristocracy and the Roman populace. Laws issued by Pompey include *Lex Pompeia* (52 B.C., concerning magisterial candidates), *Lex Pompeia* (52 B.C., concerning provincial administration), *Lex Pompeia de ambitu* (62 B.C., concerning bribery), *Lex Pompeia de parricidio* (55 or 52 B.C., concerning parricide), and *Lex Pompeia de vi* (52 B.C., concerning violence).

[10] Julius Caesar (102–44 B.C.), Roman soldier and statesman, promulgated several laws, such as the *Lex Iulia agraria* (59 B.C., agrarian law), *Lex Iulia de pecuniis mutuis* (49 B.C., debtor law), *Lex Iulia maiestatis* (46 B.C., against treason), *Lex Iulia sumptuaria* (46 B.C., against luxury), and others.

[11] Constantine I, the Great, was caesar of the Roman Empire from 306 to 325 and emperor from 325 to his death in 337.

[12] Theodosius II, the younger, was emperor of the Eastern Roman Empire (408–50). He promulgated the Theodosian code in 438 A.D.

[13] The Gregorian code was a private (that is, unofficial) code of Roman law promulgated ca. 294 A.D. by Gregorius from the law school of Beirut. It exists only in fragments.

[14] The Hermogenian code was a code of Roman law unofficially promulgated ca. 294 A.D. by Hermogenianus at Beirut. It contained the laws of Diocletian from 291 to 294. This legal code appeared to have been an addition to the Gregorian code and has survived only in fragments.

[15] "Moses . . . Theodosian code" is based on Isidore of Seville, *Etymologiae,* 5,1. The *Etymologiae (Etymologies)* were a book of universal learning, which served as an encyclopadia in the Middle Ages. Its author, Isidore of Seville (560–636), was the bishop of Seville (ca. 600–36) and an influential scholar of Visigothic Spain. An English translation of *Etymologiae,* 5,1 is available in Ernst Brehaut, *An Encyclopedist of the Dark Ages: Isidore of Seville,* Studies in History, Economics, and Public Law, 48, no. 1 (New York, 1912), pp. 166–67. For the Theodosian code, see Clyde Pharr, trans., *The Theodosian Code and Novels and the Sirmondian Constitutions* (Princeton, 1952).

[16] "Then, each people . . . common use" is based on Isidore, *Etymologiae,* 5,3 (Brehaut, *Encyclopedist,* pp. 167–68).

[17] There was no Frankish King Theoderich at the battle of Châlons (451). There was, however, the Visigothic King Theoderic I, who fought against the Huns and was killed during the battle. The reference to Theoderich is to Theuderic I, one of the four sons of Clovis and king of Metz, 511–34.

[18] In the battle of Châlons or the Catalaunian Plains (451), Attila, the Huns, and their German allies were opposed by the Roman patrician Aetius, the Franks, and the Visigoths.

[19] Childebert II, king of Austrasia, 575–96.

[20] Chlotar II (584–629) became king of all Merovingian Gaul (613–29) and was the father of Dagobert I, who continued his father's policy of extending Frankish influence to neighboring peoples.

[21] Dagobert I was king of the Merovingian Franks, 629–39.

[22] "Laws, however, are proclaimed . . . punishment" is based on Isidore, *Etymologiae,* 5,20 (Brehaut, *Encyclopedist,* p. 171).

Titles

[1] *Exercitu* (army), which is part of the law itself, makes less sense in the title. *Utilitate* (service) is used in the law, and it is employed here in the title.

[2] The reference to cutting off a hand or a foot is contained in Lex IV, 9, not in IV, 10. The title of Lex IV, 10 mistakenly confuses this with the title of IV, 9.

[3] Individual listings of laws for title V are not given in the Ingolstadt Ms., which simply gives *cap. num. VIIII.*

[4] Only *num. cap. XII* is given for title VI in the Ingolstadt Ms., in place of a list of individual laws.

[5] This title pertains to Lex VII, 1. See the law itself below.

[6] This title pertains to Lex VII, 2.

[7] This title pertains to Lex VII, 3.

[8] This title pertains to Lex VII, 3a, which is listed within the Ingolstadt Ms. as Lex I, 14.

[9] This title pertains to Lex VII, 4.

[10] Horses of inferior value are discussed in XIV, 12 along with horses of average value. The title to Lex XIV, 13 should be concerned with the cutting off of the tail or ear of an ox. See Lex XIV, 13.

[11] Most mss. assign only twenty-two titles to the Bavarian laws; the Ingolstadt Ms. is an exception. The twenty-third title concerns the illegal dispersion of another freeman's pigs. The law is supplied in this English translation and appears under its own heading. Lex XXIII, 1 appears as Lex IV, 26 in Schwind's edition.

[12] The Ingolstadt Ms. does not list laws individually for titles XX–XXII [XXIII]. In Latin, the headings for titles XX–XXIII are respectively: *cap. num. VIIII; cap. VI; cap XI; cap. I.*

Laws

[1] This preface clearly shows foreign influence in Bavaria at the time this legal code was promulgated.

[2] Later mss. add *non duc* (nor the duke).

[3] For property given to Bavarian churches and monasteries and confirmed by charters during the Carolingian age, see Theodor Bitterauf, ed., *Die Traditionen des Hochstiftes Freising, 744–1283,* Quellen und Erörterungen zur bayerischen und deutschen Geschichte, neue Folge, 4 (Munich, 1905).

[4] Later mss. add *id est novem [IX] capita restituat* (that is, let him restore it nine times).

[5] Eckhardt A gives twelve solidi.

[6] Matthew 6:14–15.

[7] Eckhardt A and Schwind give forty solidi.

[8] Beyerle, pp. lxxxviii–lxxxix believes this law may have been introduced into the Bavarian laws at the Church Synod of Dingolfing in 770.

[9] 1 Corinthians 5:13.

[10] 1 Corinthians 5:5.

[11] Like Lex I, 11, this law may have been derived from the Synod of Dingolfing (770).

[12] The title is part of the law itself. The title of Lex I, 13 in the introductory list of titles (see above) is: Concerning *coloni* and slaves of a church; how they are to serve (*De colonis et servis aeclesiae, qualiter serviant*). The title in the law given here is: Concerning *coloni* or slaves of a church: how they are to serve or how they render tribute (*De colonis vel servis aecclesiae, qualiter serviant, vel quale tributa reddant*). For a detailed study of this law, see my "Seigneurial Obligations and 'Lex Baiuvariorum' I, 13," *Traditio* 31 (1975): 336–43.

¹³ Beyerle, p. 46, n. 1 adds: *prato arpento fenum cludere secare colligere et trahere* (For an arpent [unit of land area] let him enclose the meadow and let him cut, harvest, and draw in hay).

¹⁴ The Ingolstadt Ms. lacks *poenam sustineant. . . . L percussiones accipiat* (punishment they are to endure. . . . let him receive fifty lashes). Nevertheless, Beyerle prints the missing part from other mss.

¹⁵ The retinue (*comitatis*) consisted of military followers who fought on behalf of the count. In a general sense, they may be equated with vassals fighting for their lord.

¹⁶ *centurio.*

¹⁷ *decanus.*

¹⁸ The Ingolstadt Ms. lacks *Si quis in erercitu . . . Et si ille comis neglexerit inquirere . . .* (If anyone in the army . . . And if the count neglects to inquire . . .). Beyerle prints the missing part from other mss.

¹⁹ This biblical quotation is supplied without quotation marks. It is a paraphrase of Galatians 5:15.

²⁰ *In* (within) is included in the title, but is absent from the text.

²¹ *Utilitate* (service) is absent from the title. The text uses *exercitu* (army) in addition to *utilitate.*

²² Eckhardt A and Schwind give twenty solidi.

²³ The first duke of the Agilolfinga family was Garibald I (ca. 555–95). The family ruled Bavaria until the deposition of Duke Tassilo III in 788.

²⁴ The kings in question are Merovingian. The Bavarian dukes and the Merovingian nobility were related by marriage since the sixth century.

²⁵ Eckhardt A gives 600 solidi.

²⁶ Schwind gives 960 solidi.

²⁷ Other mss. add *ubi vero illis tantum XII solidos* (where theirs is as much as twelve solidi). It is added to this translation, since the law is ambiguous without it.

²⁸ Later mss. add *sanguinem* (blood).

²⁹ Also spelled *adargrati.*

³⁰ Other mss. add *et non ligaverit* (and he does not bind him).

³¹ Later mss. add *conponat* (let him compensate).

³² Later mss. add *solidis* (solidi).

³³ Other mss. add *solidi* (solidi).

³⁴ Also spelled *lidiscarti.*

³⁵ *Simili modo* (in a similar manner) begins the second sentence in the Ingolstadt Ms., although it logically is part of the first. It is appended here to the end of the first sentence, where it belongs.

³⁶ Other mss. add *si* (if).

³⁷ Other mss. substitute *unumquemque* (each one) for *hominem unum* (one man).

[38] Also spelled *marachfalli.*

[39] This spelling is modified from what the ms. gives, *inunuuan,* although Beyerle spells it as *inunvan* in his edition.

[40] Also spelled *tautragil.*

[41] Later mss. add *dum vixit* (while he lived).

[42] Exodus 23:9; Leviticus 19:33–34.

[43] The Ingolstadt Ms. does not supply introductory descriptions of laws for title V.

[44] Schwind gives three solidi.

[45] Later mss. add *eum* (him). It is added here to facilitate the translation.

[46] The Ingolstadt Ms. renders *conponat* twice. See Beyerle, p. 84, n. 1. The word is used only once in this English translation.

[47] Introductory descriptions of laws in title VI are absent from the Ingolstadt Ms.

[48] Schwind gives three solidi.

[49] Schwind gives five solidi.

[50] Later mss. add *Si policem ei absciderit, cum IV solidis conponat* (If he cuts off his thumb, let him compensate with four solidi). Schwind gives three solidi. This addition is similar to *L. Alam.* LVII, 42.

[51] Schwind says one solidus.

[52] Schwind gives two and one-half solidi.

[53] Also spelled *tautragil.*

[54] The Ingolstadt Ms. gives both *solvat* (let him pay) and *conponat* (let him compensate). *Conponat* is deleted from this English translation.

[55] Later mss. add *et operationibus die dominico* (and work on Sunday). It is added to this translation. The addition of this phrase by later mss. justifies the addition of Lex VII, 3a, which the Ingolstadt Ms. places in title I (as Lex I, 14), with ecclesiastical law. Also in title VII, Schwind numbers Lex VII, 3a as VII, 4 and Lex VII, 4 as VII, 5.

[56] *L. Baiu.* VII, 1–3 are copied verbatim from *L. Alam.* XXXIX. No other laws in the Alamannic and Bavarian laws are identical.

[57] Exodus 20:10.

[58] Schwind says sixty solidi.

[59] Eckhardt A and Schwind give twelve solidi.

[60] Also spelled *horcrift.*

[61] Also spelled *himilzorun.*

[62] Also spelled *walcwurf.*

[63] Later mss. add *vel domino* (or to her lord).

[64] Schwind and Eckhardt A give *wanclugi,* meaning a deceptive betrothal.

[65] Eckhardt A gives forty solidi.

[66] Schwind gives fifty-three solidi and one tremissis.

⁶⁷ The Ingolstadt Ms. lacks *furaverit, solus iuret . . . fortiorem dederit* (steals, let him swear alone . . . gives strength). Beyerle supplies the missing part from other mss.

⁶⁸ The Ingolstadt Ms. lacks all of Lex IX, 3. Beyerle derives this law from other mss.

⁶⁹ Schwind gives eighty solidi.

⁷⁰ Later mss. add *suum* (his).

⁷¹ The Ingolstadt Ms. lacks *Si quis liber . . . servitio tradidit, . . .* (If any freeman . . . delivered up into slavery. . . .). It is printed in Beyerle's edition from other mss.

⁷² The Ingolstadt Ms. gives *reddat* (let him return), but it makes more sense if *perdat* (let him lose), which appears in later mss, is substituted.

⁷³ 1 Thessalonians 5:21.

⁷⁴ The Ingolstadt Ms. has *domum* (house) twice. The first appearance of the word in Lex X, 1 is deleted in this translation.

⁷⁵ Also spelled *hrevavunti*.

⁷⁶ Also spelled *parc*.

⁷⁷ Schwind gives three solidi.

⁷⁸ Also spelled *hrevavunti*.

⁷⁹ Also spelled *inunwan*. This term is spelled as *inunvam* in Beyerle's edition, although the ms. gives *inunuuam*.

⁸⁰ Later mss. add *liberi* (freeman's).

⁸¹ Later mss. add *solidis* (solidi); it is added to this English translation.

⁸² Also spelled *ezzisczun*.

⁸³ Later mss. add *quam* (which), and it is added to this translation.

⁸⁴ Later mss. add *eam* (him, that is, someone); it is added to this translation.

⁸⁵ The Ingolstadt Ms. gives *inmundiciae* (uncleanliness), although Beyerle misspells it as *immundiciae*.

⁸⁶ Beyerle says these laws were derived from the decree of 772. Lex XI, 5–7 are not, therefore, found in the Ingolstadt Ms, but are derived from later mss. Lex XI, 5 and 6 are renumbered respectively as XI, 6 and 5 in Eckhardt A. Lex XI, 5–7 are absent from Schwind.

⁸⁷ Also spelled *handelod*.

⁸⁸ Later mss. add *est* (he is).

⁸⁹ The Ingolstadt Ms. gives *oportet* (it is necessary), although Beyerle's edition renders it as *opportet*.

⁹⁰ Also spelled *decoreas*.

⁹¹ Later mss. add *vero* (however) at the beginning of this sentence.

⁹² There is no title for Lex XII, 12.

⁹³ The Ingolstadt Ms. gives *quam* (which). Later mss. give *vel* (or), which is used in this translation.

[94] The Ingolstadt Ms. gives "drives" (runs) as *conpelrit*, although Beyerle gives it as *conpellrit*.

[95] Also spelled *auursam*.

[96] The Ingolstadt Ms. confuses *voluerit* (he wishes) with *nolverit* (he does not wish). Both the law and its title have been corrected here to fit the context. Both the Schwind and the Eckhardt (A) editions render *nolverit*.

[97] This law is numbered in the Ingolstadt Ms. as 12, although it is placed between numbers 7 and 9. The assignment of number 12 is clearly a scribal error.

[98] Also spelled *marach*.

[99] Although the second half of the title of this law is associated with Lex XIV, 13 in the introductory list of titles, it belongs with Lex XIV, 12. See Titles, n. 10 above.

[100] This law in the Ingolstadt Ms. contains two occurrences of the word *non*. Only one makes sense in this sentence.

[101] The Ingolstadt Ms. lacks *Et si eum potuerit invenire . . . domino restituere non moretur* (And if he can find him . . . let him not delay to return it to the owner). This part of the law is derived from other mss.

[102] The Ingolstadt Ms. lacks Lex XV, 4–7 *in toto*. Beyerle derives these laws from other mss.

[103] The Ingolstadt Ms. lacks *Quodsi mater . . . usufructuariam* (But if a mother . . . usufruct). Beyerle derives this from other mss.

[104] Later ms. add *cum* (with); it is added to this translation.

[105] Galatians 4:30.

[106] The Ingolstadt Ms. lacks *Si autem maritus . . . illas res fiscus adquirat* (If, however, her husband . . . let the public treasury acquire these properties). Beyerle derives this from other mss.

[107] The Ingolstadt Ms. lacks Lex XVI, 1–2 *in toto*. Beyerle derives these laws from other mss.

[108] Later mss. add *testes* (witnesses); it is added to this translation.

[109] The Ingolstadt Ms. lacks *Si quis . . . firmam esse* (If anyone . . . to validate). This part of the law is derived from other mss.

[110] The Ingolstadt Ms. lacks *reddatur* (be rendered); it is added to this translation.

[111] The Ingolstadt Ms. lacks *servus* (slave); it is added here.

[112] Also spelled *cambias*.

[113] Later mss. add *istum* (that), and it is added to this translation.

[114] Freehold land, i.e., *alod*.

[115] Also spelled *farsvirotos*.

[116] Later mss. add *habeat* (is upheld); it is added to this translation.

[117] Other mss. add *an veritatem* (or truthfully), and it is added here.

[118] Later mss. add *duorum pugna et dicere: Defendere* (wager of battle and say—to defend). It is added to this translation.

[119] Other mss. add *postea donet arma sua ad sacrandum et per ea iuret ipsum verbum cum uno sacramentale* (afterwards let him give his weapons for consecration, and let him swear his words upon them with one oathtaker). This portion is added to this translation.

[120] Later mss. add *sin autem, cum* (if, however, without . . . with). It is added to this translation.

[121] Later mss. add *modo* (way), and it is added to this translation.

[122] Also spelled *walaraupa.*

[123] Later mss. place *liber sit an servus, . . . et postea repertum fuerit* (be he freeman or slave . . . and afterwards he is discovered) earlier in the text than does the Ingolstadt Ms. They are translated in agreement with later mss.

[124] Genesis 23:15.

[125] The Ingolstadt Ms. does not supply introductory descriptions of laws for title XX.

[126] The Ingolstadt Ms. gives *leitihunt,* although Beyerle spells this as *laitihunt.*

[127] Also spelled *swarzwild.*

[128] Schwind classifies *Si autem canes per vestimentum aut per membrum hominem . . . canem non requiratur* (If, moreover, a dog holds a man by his clothing or a limb . . . let him not require the new dog) as Lex XX, 10.

[129] The Ingolstadt Ms. supplies no individual introductory descriptions for title XXI.

[130] Also spelled *chranohari.*

[131] Also spelled *sparavariis.*

[132] Introductory descriptions of laws are not given in the Ingolstadt Ms. for title XXII.

[133] Later mss. delete *solidus.*

[134] Later mss. add *VI.*

[135] Later mss. place *aut ex furculis conpositum fuerit, cum pugillo termis vicibus* (or by wicker wood, let him strike the hive three times with his fist) earlier than does the Ingolstadt Ms. It is placed here in agreement with the later mss.

[136] Later mss. add *si . . . lex* (if . . . the law). This is added here.

[137] No introductory descriptions of laws in title XXIII are supplied in the Ingolstadt Ms.

[138] Lex XXIII, 1 is numbered as Lex IV, 26 in Schwind's edition.

Glossary

Many Germanic terms appear in both the Alamannic and Bavarian laws. For those Germanic terms which are peculiar to the Alamannic laws and the *Pactus legis Alamannorum,* see Georg Baesecke, "Die deutschen Worte der germanischen Gesetze," *Beiträge zur Geschichte der deutschen Sprache und Literatur* 59 (1935): 1–101. For the Germanic terms in the Bavarian laws, see Dietrich von Kralik, "Die deutschen Bestandteile der Lex Baiuvariorum," *Neues Archiv der Gesellschaft für ältere Geschichtskunde* 38 (1913): 13–55, 401–49, 581–624, and Th. von Grienberger's review of Kralik's article in *Mitteilungen des Instituts für österreichische Geschichtsforschung* 35 (1914): 154–64. For both laws, see Horst Haider Munske, *Der germanische Rechtswortschatz im Bereich der Missetaten: Philologische und sprachgeographische Untersuchungen,* Studia Linguistica germanica, 8/1 (Berlin, 1973), Vol. 1. (References to Munske are to his paragraphic divisions and not to his pagination.) Alternate spellings of terms in the Alamannic laws can be seen in Eckhardt B, pp. 86–88; alternate spellings of terms in the Bavarian laws are available in Schwind, pp. 486–89.

For the Latin terms, see J. F. Niermeyer, *Mediae latinitatis lexicon minus,* 12 fasc. (Leiden, 1954–76).

adarcrati. L. Baiu. IV, 4. A cut vein. Kralik, 405–6; Grienberger, 160; Munske, 346.

angargnago. L. Baiu. XIV, 12. "Grass-chewer," pertaining to a horse of inferior value. Kralik, 415; Grienberger, 156.

anothapuh.   L. Baiu. XXI, 3. A duck-seizing hawk. Kralik, 415.

aranscarti.   L. Baiu. XIII, 8. Injury to crops. Kralik, 415; Munske, 390.

avursam.   L. Baiu. XIV, 4. An injured animal. Kralik, 415–19; Grienberger, 155.

balebrust, paleprust.   L. Alam. LVII, 35. L. Baiu. IV, 4. A broken bone that is not a compound fracture. Baesecke, 19; Kralik, 584–87; Grienberger, 158–59; Munske, 346.

baro.   Pactus II, 10; XIV, 6; XV. L. Alam. LXIX; XCII, 4. A freeman. Niermeyer, fasc. 1 (1954), 85.

calasneo.   L. Baiu. XXII, 11. A person holding land in common with another. Kralik, 409–25; Grienberger, 156.

campias.   L. Baiu. XVI, 8. An exchange of property. Niermeyer, fasc. 2 (1955), 118 (*cambium*).

camurdrit.   L. Baiu. XIX, 3. Murder. (See *mortaudo*.) Kralik, 425.

canshapuh.   L. Baiu. XXI, 2. A goose-seizing hawk, a goshawk. Kralik, 425.

carmulum.   L. Baiu. II, 3. An insurrection. Kralik, 425–28; Grienberger, 163–64.

colonus.   L. Alam. VIII; XXII, 1; LV. L. Baiu. I, 13. An indentured free agricultural tenant. Niermeyer, fasc. 3 (1956); 203.

corf.   L. Alam. LXXXI. A clod of earth. Baesecke, 29.

cranohari.   L. Baiu. XXI, 1. A crane-seizing hawk. Kralik, 429; Grienberger, 155–56.

decorvas.   L. Baiu. XII, 4. A boundary marker in a tree. Niermeyer, fasc. 4 (1956), 308 (*decoria*).

denarius.   L. Alam. Va, 2. L. Baiu. IX, 2. A small silver coin, equated with a penny. Niermeyer, fasc. 4 (1956), 319 (*denariata*).

etorcartea.   L. Baiu. X, 17. A top pole of a fence. Kralik, 429.

ezziscgun.   L. Baiu. X, 16. A fence surrounding a wheat field. Kralik, 429–30.

farsuirotos.   L. Baiu. XVI, 17. Unjust confirmation, a false swearing. Kralik, 599–600; Grienberger, 162.

firstfalli.   L. Baiu. X, 3, 4. A roof deliberately knocked down. Kralik, 430; Grienberger, 160; Munske, 366.

firstsul.   L. Baiu. X, 7. A post supporting a roof. Kralik, 430.

fredus.   L. Alam. I, 2; III, 3; IV; V, 3; XXX; XXXI; XXXVI, 2; XXXVII, 2. L. Baiu. I, 6, 7, 9; IX, 15; XIII, 2, 3. A fine paid to the government, rendered in addition to the payment to the victim of a crime. Niermeyer, fasc. 5 (1957), 453.

frilaz, frilaza.   L. Baiu. Title V; VIII, 10. A freed person. Kralik, 430–38.

[h]aisstera [h]anti, haistera handi.   L. Alam. IX. To enter another's premises forcibly. Munske, 320.

hantalod. L. Baiu. XI, 7. A seizure. Kralik, 438; Munske, 365.

hapuhhunt. L. Baiu. XX, 6. A dog which seizes prey from a hawk. Kralik, 438.

heimzuht. L. Baiu. IV, 24. A band numbering fewer than forty-two men. Kralik, 438–39; Munske, 394.

heriraita. L. Baiu. IV, 23. A band numbering at least forty-two men. Kralik, 439; Munske, 335, 393–94.

himilzorunga. L. Baiu. VIII, 4. Raising clothes above the knees. Kralik, 439–40; Grienberger, 158; Munske, 364.

horcrif. L. Baiu. VIII, 3. Lasciviously seizing a woman. Kralik, 440; Grienberger, 157; Munske, 372.

hovawart. L. Baiu. XX, 9. A watchdog. Kralik, 441.

hraopant. L. Baiu. IV, 8. A binding, detaining another against his will. Kralik, 441–44; Grienberger, 158; Munske, 362.

hrevavunt, hrevavunta, hrevavunti, hrevovunt, revavunti. L. Alam. LVII, 55. L. Baiu. I, 6; IV, 6; V, 5; VI, 5; X, 1, 4. An internal injury. Baesecke, 35; Kralik, 445–47; Grienberger, 160; Munske, 346.

infanc. L. Baiu. IV, 3; V, 3; VI, 3. A detainment. Kralik, 447–48; Munske, 365.

inunuuam, inunwan. L. Baiu. IV, 17, 19, 21; X, 4. Endangering life. Kralik, 611–12; Grienberger, 162.

kepolsceni. L. Baiu. IV, 4. An uncovered skull, where a skull is exposed. Kralik, 448–49; Munske, 346.

laitihunt, leitihunt. L. Alam. LXXVIII, 3. L. Baiu. XX, 1. A lead dog or bloodhound. Baesecke, 18; Kralik, 449; Grienberger, 156.

lidiscart. L. Baiu. IV, 14. A disfigurement, a mutilation. Kralik, 449; Grienberger, 160; Munske, 355.

marach. L. Alam. LXI, 1; LXIII, 1. A mare. Baesecke, 18.

marca, marcha. Pactus XXXIX, 1. L. Alam. XLVI. A border, a boundary. Niermeyer, fasc. 7 (1959), 651.

marchfalli. L. Baiu. IV, 18. Thrown or pulled off a horse. Kralik, 583; Grienberger, 160; Munske, 366.

marchzand, marczan. L. Alam. LVII, 22. L. Baiu. IV, 16; VI, 10. A molar. Baesecke, 18; Kralik, 584.

marhc. L. Baiu. XIV, 11. A war horse. Kralik, 583.

minoflidus, minoflidis. Pactus XIV, 6, 9. A small landowner, that is, the lower class of freemen. Edgar H. McNeal, *Minores and Mediocres in the Germanic Tribal Laws* (Columbus, 1905), p. 56.

morgangeba. L. Alam. LIV, 3. Morning gift, that is, a gift given to the wife the morning after the wedding night. Niermeyer, fasc. 8 (1960), 705 (*morginegiva*).

mortaudo, mortaudus, murdrida. Pactus XV. L. Alam. XLVIII; LXIX. L. Baiu. XIX, 2. Murder. Baesecke, 31; Kralik, 584; Grienberger, 161; Munske, 341.

mundium. Pactus XXXV, 1. L. Alam. L, 2; LIII, 1. Guardianship of a woman. Niermeyer, fasc. 8 (1960), 709–10.

nasthait. L. Alam. LIV, 3. Taking an oath. Baesecke, 29.

parch. L. Baiu. X, 2. A granary. Kralik, 587–89.

piparhunt. L. Baiu. XX, 4. A dachshund. Kralik, 589.

plotruns. L. Baiu. IV, 2. A bloody injury. Kralik, 589; Grienberger, 159; Munske, 349.

pulislac. L. Alam. LVII, 1. L. Baiu. IV, 1; V, 1. A blow which causes swelling. Baesecke, 19; Kralik, 589–90; Grienberger, 158.

saiga. Pactus XXV, 5; XXXVIII, 2. L. Alam. Va, 1–3; XCV, 13. L. Baiu. I, 3; IX, 2; XII, 10; XIII, 4; XIV, 9, 10, 14; XVII, 2. A small gold coin, twelve of which equal one solidus. Niermeyer, fasc. 10 (1963), 930.

scardi. L. Alam. LVII, 10. A disfigurement. (See *lidiscart.*) Baesecke, 18.

scof. L. Baiu. X, 2. A storehouse without walls. Kralik, 590.

scopar. L. Baiu. X, 2. A small farm storehouse. Kralik, 590.

selisohan. L. Baiu, XI, 5. A house search. Kralik, 590–91; Grienberger, 161; Munske, 394.

solidus. Pactus, L. Alam., L. Baiu., *passim.* A gold coin, equal to three tremisses or twelve saigae. Niermeyer, fasc. 11 (1964), 978.

spanga. L. Baiu. X, 13. An outside beam which holds the walls of a building together. Kralik, 591.

sparawaris. L. Baiu. XXI, 4. A sparrow hawk. Kralik, 36–37.

spurihunt. L. Baiu. XX, 3. A bloodhound. Kralik, 591; Grienberger, 156.

suarzwild. L. Baiu. XX, 7. "Black animals," meaning large wild animals. Kralik, 597–98.

suezcholi. L. Baiu. XIV, 15. A blood disease. Kralik, 598–99; Grienberger, 160.

suiron. L. Baiu. XIV, 12. To swear, to confirm. (See *farsuirotos.*) Kralik, 599–601.

taudregil, tautragil. L. Alam. LVII, 62. L. Baiu. IV, 27; VI, 11. Being lame. Baesecke, 19; Kralik, 601–3; Grienberger, 156.

tremissis. Pactus II, 8; XVI, 2; XVII, 3, 6; XXIV, 1; XXXVIII, 1, 5. L. Alam. Va, 2; XXI; LXVIII, 2; LXXI, 1, 2; LXXXVI, 2–4; XCII, 2; XCV, 7. L. Baiu. I, 3, 13; II, 15; IV, 11; IX, 2, 12; XIII, 4; XIV, 9, 12, 13; XXII, 3, 4. A gold coin, three of which equal one solidus. Niermeyer, fasc. 11 (1964), 1040.

triphunt. L. Baiu. XX, 2. A bloodhound. Kralik, 603.

untprut. L. Baiu. XXII, 10. Removing another's property. Kralik, 604–11; Grienberger, 159.

valuraupa. L. Baiu. XIX, 4. Robbery of clothing from the dead. Kralik, 615–16; Grienberger, 155; Munske, 385.

walcuurf. L. Baiu. VIII, 5. A head covering. Kralik, 613–15; Grienberger, 158; Munske, 364.

wancstodal. L. Baiu. IV, 26; VIII, 17. A deceptive situation. Kralik, 618–19; Grienberger, 161–62; Munske, 360.

wegalaugen. Pactus XVIII, 1. A waylayer. Baesecke, 37; Munske, 360.

wehadinc. L. Baiu. XII, 8. A wager of battle, a trial of combat. Kralik, 619–21; Grienberger, 157.

wergeld. Pactus XIV, 5; XV; XXVIII, 1, 2; XXIX, 1; XXXII, 1; XXXIX, 2. L. Alam. IV; XXVIII, 1; XXXIV, 1; XLIV, 1, 2; XLV; XLVIII; XLIX, 1; L, 2; LIII, 2; LXI, 1; LXII, 1; LXIX; XCVI, 3, 4; XCVII, 4. L. Baiu. VIII, 1, 2, 19; IX, 4; XVI, 5; XIX, 2. The price of a person's life, computed in money, which varied according to his class (slave, freed, free). Kralik, 38–41.

wiffam. L. Baiu. X, 18. A sign or marker placed in the ground. Kralik, 621; Grienberger, 155.

wilz. L. Baiu. XIV, 12. A horse of average value. Kralik, 621–22; Grienberger, 156.

winchilsul. L. Baiu. X, 8. An inside post. Kralik, 622.

zauganzuht. L. Baiu. XI, 6. Proof of property ownership. Kralik, 622–23.

Bibliography

LEGAL

This bibliography contains only recent editions and criticism of the Alamannic and Bavarian laws. For older material, see Heinrich Brunner, *Deutsche Rechtsgeschichte,* 2d ed. 2 vols. (Leipzig, 1906–28), 1:448 (*Pactus* and Alamannic laws) and 454 (Bavarian laws).

Alamannic laws

Editions

Eckhardt, Karl August, ed. and trans. *Germanenrechte Texte und Übersetzungen.* Vol. 2, *Die Gesetze des Karolingerreiches.* pt. 2: *Alemannen und Bayern.* Weimar, 1934. *Lex Alamannorum* appears in Volume 2, pt. 2, pp. 1–71.
———, ed. *Leges Alamannorum.* 1 and 2. Germanenrechte Neue Folge, Westgermanisches Recht, 6–7. Vol. 1: Göttingen, 1958. Vol. 2: Witzenhausen, 1962.
Lehmann, Karl, ed. *Leges Alamannorum. Monumenta Germaniae Historica.* Legum Sectio 1, Vol. 5, pt. 1. Rev. ed., Karl August Eckhardt. Hanover, 1966. (Lehmann's edition originally appeared in 1888.)

Criticism

Beyerle, Franz. "Die beiden süddeutschen Stammesrechte." *Zeitschrift der Savigny-Stiftung für Rechtsgeschichte, Germanistische Abteilung* 73 (1956): 84–140.

————. "Das Kulturporträt die beiden süddeutschen Rechtstexte: Pactus und Lex Alamannorum." *Hegau* 2 (1956): 93–108.

————. "Die süddeutschen Leges und die merowingische Gesetzgebung. Volksrechtliche Studien II." *Zeitschrift der Savigny-Stiftung für Rechtsgeschichte, Germanistische Abteilung* 49 (1929): 264–432.

Bonin, Burkhard von. "Zu Pactus Alamannorum III, 3–4." *Neues Archiv der Gesellschaft für ältere deutsche Geschichtskunde* 30 (1905): 143–44.

Brunner, Heinrich. "Über das Alter der Lex Alamannorum." *Sitzungsberichte der Berliner Akademie der Wissenschaften* 8 (1885): 149–72. Reprinted in his *Abhandlungen zur Rechtsgeschichte: Gesammelte Aufsätze,* edited by Karl Rauch. 2 vols. Weimar, 1931. Vol. 1: 569–98.

————. "Über ein verschollenes merowingisches Königsgesetz des 7. Jahrhunderts." *Sitzungsberichte der Berliner Akademie der Wissenschaften* 39 (1901): 932–55. Reprinted in his *Abhandlungen,* 1: 598–628.

Buchner, Rudolf. *Die Rechtsquellen,* Beiheft in W. Wattenbach and Wilhelm Levison, *Deutschlands Geschichtsquellen im Mittelalter, Vorzeit und Karolinger.* Weimar, 1953. Pp. 29–33.

Dölling, Hildegard. *Haus und Hof in westgermanischen Volksrechten.* Veröffentliche der Altertumskommission im Provinzialinstitut für westfälische Landes- und Volkskunde, 2. Münster, 1958. "Haus und Hof nach der Lex Alamannorum," pp. 27–32.

Fehr, Hans. "Der Geist der alemannischen Volksrechte." *Schweizer Beiträge zur allgemeinen Geschichte* 1 (1943): 34–54.

Koehne, Karl. "Der 'faber publice probatus' der Lex Alam. LXXIV, 5." *Vierteljahrschrift für Sozial- und Wirtschaftsgeschichte* 4 (1906): 186–90.

Krusch, Bruno. *Die Lex Bajuvariorum. Textgeschichte. Handschriftenkritik und Entstehung. Mit zwei Anhängen: Lex Alamannorum und Lex Ribuaria.* Berlin, 1924.

————. *Neue Forschungen über die drei oberdeutschen Leges: Bajuvariorum, Alamannorum, Ribuariorum, etc.* Abhandlungen der Gesellschaft der Wissenschaften zu Göttingen, phil.-hist. Klasse, neue Folge, 20, no. 1. Berlin, 1927.

Kudrna, Jaroslav. *Studie k barbarským zákoníkum 'Lex Baiuvariorum' a 'Lex Alamanorum' a počátkum feudáiních vztahu v jižním Německu.* Spisky University v Brně filosofická fakulta. Cislo, 60. Prague, 1959.

Lear, Floyd Seyward. "The Public Law of the Ripuarian, Alamannic, and Bavarian Codes." *Medievalia et Humanistica* 2 (1944): 3–27. Reprinted in his *Treason in Roman and Germanic Law: Collected Papers.* Austin, 1965. Pp. 196–226.

Mayer, Ernst. *Die oberdeutschen Volksrechte.* Leipzig, 1929.

Rivers, Theodore John. "Contributions to the Criticism and Interpretation of the 'Lex Baiuvariorum': A Comparative Study of the Alamannic and Bavarian Codes." Ph.D. dissertation, Fordham University, 1973.

————. "The Legal Status of Freewomen in the Lex Alamannorum." *Zeitschrift der Savigny-Stiftung für Rechtsgeschichte, Germanistische Abteilung* 91 (1974): 175–79.

Schott, Clausdieter. "Pactus, Lex und Recht." In *Die Alemannen in der Frühzeit,* edited by Wolfgang Hübener. Veröffentlichung des Alemannischen Instituts Freiburg im Breisgau, 34. Bühl & Baden, 1974. Pp. 135–68.

Vismara, Giulio. "Cristianesimo e legislazioni germaniche: leggi longobarde, alamanne e bavare." In *La conversione al cristianesimo nell' Europa dell' alto medioevo.* Settimane di studio del centro italiano di studi sull' alto medioevo, 14. Spoleto, 1967. Pp. 397–467.

Ziebermayr, Ignaz. *Noricum, Baiern und Österreich: Lorsch als Hauptstadt und die Einführung des Christentums.* 2d ed. Horn, 1956. Ch. 15, "Die Volksrechte der Baiern und Alamannen und das Christentum." Pp. 211–28.

Bavarian laws

Editions

Beyerle, Konrad, ed. and trans. *Lex Baiuvariorum: Lichtdruck Wiedergabe der Ingolstädter Handschrift des bayerischen Volksrechts.* Munich, 1926.

Eckhardt, Karl August, ed. and trans. *Germanenrechte Texte und Übersetzungen.* Vol. 2, *Die Gesetze des Karolingerreiches.* Pt. 2: *Alemannen und Bayern.* Weimar, 1934. *Lex Baiuvariorum* appears in Volume 2, pt. 2, pp. 73–183.

Riesinger, Hubert, ed. and trans. *Die Lex Baiuvariorum: Eine Auswahl mit Einleitung und Erläuterungen.* Straubinger Heft, 4. Humanistisches Gymnasium und Ludwigs-Oberrealschule. Straubing, 1954. German translation, in part, appears on pp. 9–26. Reprinted in *Beilage zur Amtl. Schul.-Abz. für dem Reg.-Bez. Niederbayern,* 1959, no. 5. Pp. 59–102.

Schwind, Ernst von. ed. *Lex Baiwariorum. Monumenta Germaniae Historica.* Legum Sectio 1, Vol. 5, pt. 2. Hanover, 1926.

Criticism

Bauerreiss, Romuald. "Benediktinerregel und Lex Baiuvariorum." *Studien und Mitteilungen zur Geschichte des Benediktiner-Ordens und seiner Zweige* 61 (1947): 73–76.

Beyerle, Franz. "Die beiden süddeutschen Stammesrechte."

———. "Die süddeutschen Leges."

———. Review of Bruno Krusch, *Die Lex Bajuvariorum. Textgeschichte, Handschriftenkritik und Entstehung. Mit zwei Anhängen: Lex Alamannorum und Lex Ribuaria* (Berlin, 1924). *Zeitschrift der Savigny-Stiftung für Rechtsgeschichte, Germanistische Abteilung* 44 (1925): 416–57.

Brunner, Heinrich. "Merovingisches Königsgesetz."

Buchner, Rudolf. *Die Rechtsquellen.* Pp. 26–29.

Dölling, Hildegard. *Haus und Hof.* "Haus und Hof nach der Lex Baiuvariorum," pp. 19–27.

Eckhardt, Karl August. *Die Lex Baiuvariorum. Eine textkritische Studie.* Untersuchungen zur deutschen Staats- und Rechtsgeschichte, 138. Breslau, 1927.

Gebhard, Torsten. "Zu den Hausangaben der lex Bajuvariorum." *Germania* 29 (1951): 230–35.

Grienberger, Th. von. Review of Dietrich von Kralik, "Die deutschen Bestandteile der Lex Baiuvariorum" (*Neues Archiv der Gesellschaft für ältere deutsche Geschichtskunde* 38 [1913]: 13–55, 401–49, 581–624). *Mitteilungen des Instituts für österreichische Geschichtsforschung* 35 (1914): 154–64.

Heymann, Ernst. "Zur Textkritik der Lex Bajuwariorum." In *Papsttum und Kaisertum, Paul Kehr dargebracht,* edited by Albert Brachmann. Munich, 1926. Pp. 116–37.

Hohenlohe, K. *Das Kirchenrecht der Lex Bajuwariorum.* Vienna, 1932.

Kralik, Dietrich von. "Die deutschen Bestandteile der Lex Baiuvariorum." *Neues Archiv der Gesellschaft für ältere deutsche Geschichtskunde* 38 (1913): 13–55, 401–49, 581–624.

Krause, Hermann. "Die Liberi der lex Baiuvariorum." In *Festschrift für Max Spindler zum 75. Geburtstag,* edited by Dieter Albrecht, Andreas Kraus, and Kurt Reindel. Munich, 1969. Pp. 41–73.

Krusch, Bruno. *Die Lex Bajuvariorum.*

———. *Neue Forschungen.*

Kudrna, Jaroslav. *Studie k barbarským zákoníkum.*

Lear, Floyd Seyward. "Ripuarian, Alamannic and Bavarian Codes."

Mayer, Ernst. *Die oberdeutschen Volksrechte.*

Metz, Wolfgang. "Die hofrechtlichen Bestimmungen der Lex Baiuvariorum I, 13 und die fränkische Reichsgutverwaltung." *Deutsches Archiv für Geschichte des Mittelalters* 12 (1956): 187–96.

Paringer, P. Benedikt. "Zur Textgeschichte der Lex Baiuvariorum." *Der Zweibelturm* 8 (1953): 23–25.

Reindel, Kurt. "Die Entstehung der *Lex Baiuvariorum.*" *Unser Bayern* (supplement to *Bayerische Staatszeitung*) 6 (1957), no. 9.

———. "Neue Forschungen zur *Lex Baiuvariorum.*" *Zeitschrift für bayerische Landesgeschichte* 21 (1958): 130–37.

————. "Recht und Verfassung." In *Handbuch der bayerischen Geschichte,* edited by Max Spindler. Munich, 1967. Pp. 171–79.

Rivers, Theodore John. "Contributions."

————. "Seigneurial Obligations and 'Lex Baiuvariorum' I, 13." *Traditio* 31 (1975): 336–43.

Schnetz, Josef. "Andecena, Andecinga." *Mitteilungen des Instituts für österreichische Geschichtsforschung* 45 (1930): 347–49.

————. "Das Flächenmass *andecena, andecinga* der *Lex Baiuvariorum.* Sprachliche Darlegung." *Zeitschrift für bayerische Landesgeschichte* 4 (1931): 75–80.

Schwind, Ernst von. "Kritische Studien zur Lex Baiuvariorum." *Neues Archiv der Gesellschaft für ältere deutsche Geschichtskunde* 31 (1906): 399–453; 33 (1908): 605–94; 37 (1912): 415–51.

Strecker, Karl. "Baioaria Lex." *Neues Archiv der Gesellschaft für ältere deutsche Geschichtskunde* 46 (1925/26): 513–15.

Vismara, Giulio, "Cristianesimo e legislazioni germaniche."

Zeller, Friedrich. *Das Verhältnis der Lex Bajuwariorum zum späteren bayerischen Recht: Ein Beitrag zur Kritik des bayerische Volksrechts.* Jur. D. dissertation. Munich, 1941.

Ziebermayr, Ignaz. "Die Volksrechte."

HISTORICAL

This bibliography cites historical, cultural, and archaeological scholarship on the Germanic kingdoms in general and the Alamans and Bavarians in particular. It makes no pretense to being exhaustive.

Germanic Kingdoms

Bachrach, Bernard S. *Merovingian Military Organization, 481–751.* Minneapolis, 1972.

Bognetti, Gian Piero. *L'età longobarda.* 4 vols. Milan, 1966–68.

Bury, J. B. *The Invasion of Europe by the Barbarians.* London, 1928.

Courcelle, Pierre. *Histoire littéraire des grandes invasions germaniques.* 3d ed. Paris, 1964.

Courtois, Christian. *Les Vandales et l'Afrique.* Paris, 1955.

Crawford, S. J. *Anglo-Saxon Influence on Western Christendom, 600–800.* Oxford, 1933.

Dalton, O. M. *The History of the Franks by Gregory of Tours.* 2 vols. Oxford, 1927.

Dill, Samuel. *Roman Society in Gaul in the Merovingian Age.* London, 1926.

Dopsch, Alfons. *The Economic and Social Foundations of European Civilization.* Translated by M. G. Beard and Nadine Marshall. London, 1937.

Ensslin, Wilhelm. *Theoderich der Grosse.* 2d ed. Munich, 1959.

Goebel, Julius, Jr. *Felony and Misdemeanor: A Study in the History of English Criminal Procedure.* Research in Legal History, Columbia University School of Law, 1. New York, 1937.

Graus, F. X. *Volk, Herrscher und Heiliger im Reich der Merowinger.* Prague, 1965.

Grierson, Philip. "Election and Inheritance in Early Germanic Kingship." *The Cambridge Historical Journal* 7 (1941/43): 1–22.

Hodgkin, Thomas. *Italy and her Invaders.* 8 vols. Oxford, 1880–99.

King, P. D. *Law and Society in the Visigothic Kingdom.* Cambridge Studies in Medieval Life and Thought. Third Series, 5. Cambridge, 1972.

Lasko, Peter. *The Kingdom of the Franks: North-west Europe before Charlemagne.* London, 1971.

Latouche, Robert. *The Birth of Western Economy: Economic Aspects of the Dark Ages.* Translated by E. M. Wilkinson. London, 1961.

Levison, Wilhelm. *England and the Continent in the Eighth Century.* Oxford, 1946.

Lot, Ferdinand. *The End of the Ancient World and the Beginnings of the Middle Ages.* Translated by Philip and Mariette Leon. New York, 1931.

Musset, Lucien. *The Germanic Invasions: The Making of Europe, A.D. 400–600.* Translated by Edward and Columba James. University Park, 1975.

Owen, Francis. *The Germanic People: Their Origin, Expansion and Culture.* New Haven, 1960.

Perrin, Odet. *Les Burgondes: Leur histoire, des origines à la fin du permier royaume (534).* Neuchâtel, 1968.

Pirenne, Henri. *Mohammed and Charlemagne.* Translated by Bernard Miall from 10th French ed. London, 1939.

Riché, Pierre. *Education et culture dans l'Occident barbare VIe–VIIIe siècles.* Paris, 1962.

Salin, Edouard. *La civilisation mérovingienne.* 4 vols. Paris, 1949–59.

Stenton, Frank M. *Anglo-Saxon England.* Oxford History of England, 2. 3d ed. Oxford, 1971.

Stevens, C.E. *Sidonius Apollinaris and his Age.* Oxford, 1933.

Thompson, E.A. *The Goths in Spain.* Oxford, 1969.

Wallace-Hadrill, J. M. *The Barbarian West, 400–1000.* 3d ed. London, 1967.

———. *Early Germanic Kingship in England and on the Continent.* Oxford, 1971.

———. *The Long-Haired Kings and Other Studies in Frankish History.* London, 1962.

————. ed. and trans. *The Fourth Book of the Chronicle of Fredegar with its Continuations*. London, 1960.

Alamans

Büttner, Heinrich. "Christentum und fränkischer Staat in Alemannien und Rätien während des 8. Jahrhunderts." *Zeitschrift für schweizerische Kirchengeschichte* 43 (1949): 1–27, 132–50.
————. "Christentum und Kirche zwischen Neckar und Main im 7. und frühen 8. Jahrhundert." In *Sankt Bonifatius: Gedenkgabe zum zwölfhundertsten Todestag*. 2d ed. Fulda, 1954. Pp. 362–87.

Christlein, Rainer. *Das alamannische Gräberfeld von Dirlewang bei Mindelheim*. Materialhefte zur bayerischen Vorgeschichte, 25. Kallmünz, 1971.

Dahn, Felix. *Die Könige der Germanen*. Vol. 9, pt. 1: *Die Alamannen*. Leipzig, 1902.

Feger, Otto. "Zur Geschichte des alemannischen Herzogtums." *Zeitschrift für Württembergische Landesgeschichte* 16 (1957): 41–94.

Fingerlin, Gerhard. *Die alamannischen Gräberfeld von Güttingen und Merdingen in Südbaden*. 2 vols. Germanische Denkmäler der Völkerwanderungszeit, Serie A, 12. Berlin, 1971.

Garscha, Friedrich. *Die Alamannen in Südbaden: Katalog der Grabfunde*. 2 vols. Germanische Denkmäler der Völkerwanderungszeit, Serie A, 11. Berlin, 1970.

Guyan, Walter Ulrich. *Das alamannische Gräberfeld von Schleitheim-Hebsack*. Materialhefte zur Ur- und Frühgeschichte der Schweiz, 5. Basel, 1965.

Hlawitschka, Eduard. *Franken, Alemannen, Bayern und Burgunder in Oberitalien (774–962)*. Forschungen zur Oberrheinischen Landesgeschichte, 8. Freiburg im Breisgau, 1960.

Hübener, Wolfgang, ed. *Die Alemannen in der Frühzeit*. Veröffentlichung des Alemannischen Instituts Freiburg im Breisgau, 34. Bühl and Baden, 1974.

Marti, Otto. *Römer und Alamannen am Ober-Rhein im 4. und 5. Jahrhundert n. Chr*. Bern, 1954.

Maurer, Friedrich. *Nordgermanen und Alemannen: Studien zur germanischen und frühdeutschen Sprachgeschichte, Stammes- und Volkskunde*. Bibliotheca Germanica, 3. 3d rev. ed. Bern, 1952.

Müller, P. Iso. "Zur rätisch-alemannischen Kirchengeschichte des 8. Jahrhunderts." *Schweizerische Zeitschrift für Geschichte* 2 (1952): 1–40.

Müller, W., ed. *Zur Geschichte der Alemannen*. Wege der Forschung, 100. Darmstadt, 1975.

Neuscheler, Eugen. "Ammianus Marcellinus als Quelle für die Ala-mannengeschichte." In *Festgabe für Karl Bohenberger,* edited by Hans Bihl. Tübingen, 1938. Pp. 40–52.

Paulsen, Peter. *Alamannische Adelsgräber von Niederstotzinger (Kreis Heidenheim).* Veröffentlichungen des Staatlichen Amtes für Denkmalpflege Stuttgart, Reihe A. 2 vols. Stuttgart, 1967.

————. "Die Anfänge des Christentums bei den Alamannen." *Zeitschrift für Württembergische Landesgeschichte* 15 (1956): 1–24.

Schmidt, Ludwig. *Geschichte der deutschen Stämme bis zum Ausgang der Völkerwanderung.* 2d ed. 2 vols. Munich, 1938–41. Vol. 2: *Die Westgermanen.* 2d ed. Munich, 1938–40. Esp. pp. 223–314.

Schwarz, Ernst. "Die Herkunft der Alemannen." *Vorträge und Forschungen* 1 [*Grundfragen der alemannischen Geschichte*] (1952): 37–51.

Siegwart, Josef. "Zur Frage des alemannischen Herzogsgutes um Zürich." *Schweizerische Zeitschrift für Geschichte* 8 (1958): 145–92.

Tschumi, Otto. *Burgunder, Alamannen und Langobarden in der Schweiz.* Bern, 1945.

Van der Vijner, A. "La victoire contre les Alamans et la conversion de Clovis." *Revue belge de philologie et d'histoire* 15 (1936): 859–914; 16 (1937): 35–94.

Veeck, Walther. *Die Alamannen in Württemberg.* 2 vols. Germanische Denkmäler der Völkerwanderungszeit, Serie A, 1. Berlin, 1931.

Wais, Gerhard Julius. *Die Alamannen in ihrer Auseinandersetzung mit der römischen Welt.* 3d ed. Berlin, 1943.

Weller, Karl. *Besiedlungsgeschichte Württembergs vom 3. bis 13. Jahrhundert n. Chr.* Besiedlungsgeschichte Württembergs, 3. Stuttgart, 1938. Esp. pp. 12–213.

————. *Geschichte des schwäbischen Stammes bis zum Untergang der Staufer.* Munich and Berlin, 1944. Esp. pp. 1–126.

Zöllner, Erich. *Geschichte der Franken bis zur Mitte des 6. Jahrhunderts.* Munich, 1970.

Bavarians

Bauerreiss, Romuald. *Kirchengeschichte Bayerns.* 7 vols. St. Ottilien and Augsburg, 1949–70. 2d ed., 1958. Esp. Vol. 1.

Bosl, Karl. "Das bayerische Stammesherzogtum." *Zeitschrift für bayerische Landesgeschichte* 25 (1962): 275–82. Reprinted in *Zur Geschichte der Bayern,* edited by Karl Bosl. Wege der Forschung, 60. Darmstadt, 1965. Pp. 1–11.

Dahn, Felix. *Die Könige der Germanen.* Vol. 9, pt. 2: *Die Bayern.* Leipzig, 1905.

Dannheimer, Hermann. "Reihengräber und Ortsnamen als Quelle zur frühmittelalterlichen Besiedlungsgeschichte Bayerns." In *Aus Bayerns Frühzeit: Friedrich Wagner zum 75. Geburtstag.* Schriftenreihe zur bayerischen Landesgeschichte, 62. Munich, 1962. Pp. 251–86.

Dünningen, Eberhard. *Die christliche Frühzeit Bayerns.* Munich, 1966.

Eberl, Bartholomäus. *Die Bajuwaren: Feststellungen und Fragestellungen zur Frühgeschichte des Baiernvolkes,* edited by Ingo Schaefer und Kurt Reindel. Studien zur Geschichte des Bayerischen Schwabens, Reihe 1, 11. Augsburg, 1966.

Gutmann, Franz. *Die soziale Gliederung der Bayern zur Zeit der Volksrechtes.* Abhandlungen aus dem staatswissenschaftliche Seminar zu Strasburg, 20. Strasbourg, 1906.

Hlawitschka, Eduard. *Franken, Alemannen, Bayern und Burgunder.*

Klebel, Ernst. "Zur Geschichte des Herzogs Theodo." *Verhandlungen des Historischen Vereins für Oberpfalz und Regensburg* 99 (1958): 165–205. Reprinted in *Zur Geschichte der Bayern,* edited by Karl Bosl. Wege der Forschung, 60. Darmstadt, 1965. Pp. 172–224.

Löwe, Heinz, "Bonifatius und die bayerisch-fränkische Spannung: Ein Beitrag zur Geschichte der Beziehungen zwischen dem Papsttum und den Karolingern." *Jahrbüch für fränkische Landesforschung* 15 (1955): 85–127. Reprinted in *Zur Geschichte der Bayern,* edited by Karl Bosl. Wege der Forschung, 60. Darmstadt, 1965. Pp. 264–328.

Mayr, Gottfried. *Studien zum Adel im frühmittelalterlichen Bayern.* Studien zur bayerischen Verfassungs- und Sozialgeschichte, 5. Munich, 1974.

Prinz, Friedrich. "Herzog und Adel im Agilulfingischen Bayern. Herzogsgut und Konsenschenkungen vor 788." *Zeitschrift für bayerische Landesgeschichte* 25 (1962): 283–311. Reprinted in *Zur Geschichte der Bayern,* edited by Karl Bosl. Wege der Forschung, 60. Darmstadt, 1965. Pp. 225–63.

Reiffenstein, Ingo. *Das Althochdeutsche und die irische Mission im oberdeutschen Raum.* Innsbrucker Beiträge zur Kulturwissenschaft. Sonderheft, 6. Innsbruck, 1958.

Reindel, Kurt. "Bayern im Karolingerreich." In *Karl der Grosse: Lebenswerk und Nachleben,* edited by Wolfgang Braunfels. 1: *Persönlichkeit und Geschichte.* Düsseldorf, 1965. Pp. 220–46.

———. *Bayern im Mittelalter.* Munich, 1970. Esp. pp. 9–91.

———. "Die politische Entwicklung." In *Handbuch der bayerischen Geschichte,* edited by Max Spindler. Munich, 1967, Pp. 73–133.

Riesler, Sigmund von. *Geschichte Baierns.* 2d ed. Stuttgart, 1927. Esp. 1: 3–337.

Schmidt, Ludwig. *Die Westgermanen.* Esp. pp. 128–206.

Schrott, Ludwig. *Die Herrscher Bayerns: Vom ersten Herzog bis zum letzten König.* 2d ed. Munich, 1967. Esp. pp. 13–28.

Schwarz, Ernst. "Herkunft und Einwanderungszeit der Baiern." *Südost-Forschungen* 12 (1953): 21–47.

Störmer, Wilhelm. *Adelsgruppen im früh- und hochmittelalterlichen Bayern.* Studien zur bayerischen Verfassungs- und Sozialgeschichte, 4. Munich, 1972.

Ziebermayr, Ignaz. *Noricum, Baiern und Österreich: Lorsch als Hauptstadt und die Einführung des Christentums.* 2d ed. Horn, 1956.

Zöllner, Erich. "Der bairische Adel und die Gründung von Innichen." *Mitteilungen des Instituts für österreichische Geschichtsforschung* 68 (1960): 362–87. Reprinted in *Zur Geschichte der Bayern,* edited by Karl Bosl. Wege der Forschung, 60. Darmstadt, 1965. Pp. 135–71.

———. "Die Herkunft der Agilulfinger." *Mitteilungen des Instituts für österreichische Geschichtsforschung* 59 (1951): 245–64. Reprinted in *Zur Geschichte der Bayern,* edited by Karl Bosl. Wege der Forschung, 60. Darmstadt, 1965. Pp. 107–34.

Index

197

object, sacred (*capsa*). L. Alam. Va, 4

Old Testament. L. Baiu. XV, 9

orchard. L. Baiu. title XXII; IX, 13. *See also* grove

organs, internal. L. Alam. LVII, 54, 55. L. Baiu. IV, 6; V, 5; VI, 5. *See also* intestines

ornament. L. Baiu. XV, 2; XVI, 11

ounce. L. Baiu. I, 2

oven. L. Alam. LXXVII, 1. *See also* lime oven

ox. Pactus XXIX, 1. L. Alam. VI; LXXI, 1–3; XCVI, 4. L. Baiu. I, 3, 13; VII, 3a [I, 14]; IX, 2, 10, 12; XIV, 8 [12]; XIV, 9, 13

pagan. L. Alam. XXXVII, 1

palm. L. Alam. LVII, 45, 48

parish. L. Alam. X; XII. L. Baiu. I, 9

pastor. L. Alam. VI; XI; XIX

pasture. L. Baiu. X, 18. *See also* meadow.

paten. L. Baiu. I, 3

payment, monetary
—eightfold. Pactus XXV, 4; XL, 7. L. Alam. XCV, 12
—fourfold. L. Baiu. III, 1; XV, 3
—ninefold. Pactus XV; XXIII, 6; XXIV, 5; XXV, 6; XXVI, 2. L. Alam. V, 1; LXV, 1; XCV, 6, 10, 13, 15. L. Baiu. I, 3; II, 12; IX, 1, 7
—ninefold times nine. L. Alam. XXVI, 1
—threefold. Pactus XXII, 3. L. Alam. VII; X; XI; XII; XX; XXV, 2; XXVIII, 2, 3; XXIX; XXXI; XXXII; XXXIII; XXXIV, 1, 2; XCIV, 5. L. Baiu. I, 9; XVII, 2
—thrice ninefold. L. Alam. V, 1; VI; XXVI, 2; XXXI. L. Baiu. I, 3; II, 12; IX, 2
—twofold. Pactus XXII, 4. L. Alam. XIII; XXX; XLVIII; LVI, 2; LIX, 2; LX, 2; XCIV, 6. L. Baiu. I, 8, 11; II, 17; IV, 29, 30; XIV, 16; XVI, 4, 5; XVII, 2; XIX, 4

peck. L. Baiu. I, 13

physician. Pactus I, 2, 3. L. Alam. LVII, 5, 7. L. Baiu. V, 3

pigs. Pactus XXI, 1; XXII, 1; XXIX, 1; XXXVII, 2. L. Alam. XXI; LXXII; XCIV, 1, 4; XCVI, 4. L. Baiu. title XXIII; XIII, 4; XIV, 17; XIX, 7

pigsty. L. Alam. LXXVII, 1

planks. L. Baiu. X, 14

pledge, -s. Pactus XXII, 1; XXXVII, 1. L. Alam. III, 1; XXXVI, 2; LXVII, 1; LXXXIII, 1, 2; XCIV, 4. L. Baiu. title XIII; I, 4; IV, 25; XI, 4; XVI, 17; XVII, 3

poison. Pactus XIII, 1; XIV, 1. L. Baiu. IV, 22; VIII, 18. *See also* arrow, poisoned

pole, fence. L. Baiu. X, 17. *See also* post, fence

pollution, water. L. Baiu. X, 22, 23

Pompeius. L. Baiu. prologue

post, fence. L. Baiu. X, 7–11; XIV, 11

Postumius. L. Baiu. prologue

potion. L. Baiu. IV, 22; VIII, 18. *See also* poison

priest. L. Alam. I, 1; II, 1; III, 1, 2; VI; X; XI; XII; XVIII; XIX; XX. L. Baiu. I, 1, 3, 7, 9, 12

province. L. Alam. VII; XXIX; XXXV, 1; XXXVI, 1, 2; XXXVII, 1, 2; XLV; XLVII. L. Baiu. I, 9–11, 13; II, 1, 3–5, 8, 14; IV, 30; IX, 14

puppy. L. Alam. LXXVIII, 6. *See also* dog

putrefaction. Pactus XXVIII, 2. L. Alam. XCVI, 3

quarrel. L. Alam. XXV, 1; XXXIII. *See also* dispute

rabbit. L. Baiu. XX, 5

raven. Pactus XXVI, 3. L. Alam. XCV, 16

relatives. Pactus XIV, 1; XVII, 1, 3; XXXIV, 1. L. Alam. II, 1; IV; XI; XV, 1, 2; XVII, 2; XL; XLV; LIV, 1, 2; LX, 1, 3. L. Baiu. IV, 28, 31; VIII, 9–11, 14–15; IX, 4; XV, 10; XVI, 5; XIX, 1, 7. *See also* kindred

representative, count's. L. Alam. XXXVI, 1–3